Francesca Walsh, Kerry Young, Ia
Robert Ratford, Pete Harwood, Nathan Goo

# ESSENTIALS
## AQA GCSE
## Additional Science

# Contents

# Contents

## Unit 1: Biology 2

## Unit 2: Chemistry 2

## Unit 3: Physics 2

*N.B. The numbers in brackets correspond to the reference numbers on the AQA GCSE Additional Science specification.*

# B2 | Cells and Simple Cell Transport

1. Complete the table below with a tick (✓) or cross (✗) to show if the structures are present or absent in the cells listed. One has been done for you. (3 marks)

| Structure/type of cell | Nucleus | Cytoplasm | Cell membrane | Cell wall |
|---|---|---|---|---|
| Plant cell | | | | |
| Bacterial cell | ✗ | | | |
| Animal cell | | | | |

2. Some cells are specialised to carry out a specific function. Match the cell descriptions in List A to the corresponding functions in List B. In each case, draw a line between the two. (3 marks)

**List A**

The cell has hair-like structures

The cell is very large

This cell has a tail

This cell can be very long with branched endings

**List B**

To act as a food supply

To carry nerve impulses

To absorb water

To swim

3. The drawing shows a specialised cell.

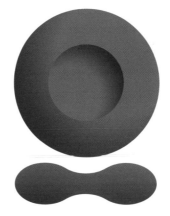

(a) What is the name of this cell? (1 mark)

(b) Suggest a reason why this cell does not have a nucleus. (1 mark)

**4.** Fiona and Issac are studying a diagram of a single-celled organism called Euglena.

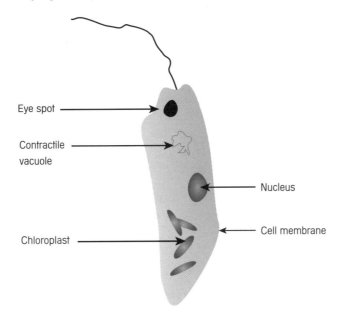

Eye spot

Contractile vacuole

Nucleus

Cell membrane

Chloroplast

**(a)** Fiona thinks Euglena is a plant cell. Give **one** reason why she might think this. (1 mark)

.................................................................................................................................................................

**(b)** Issac says that Euglena cannot be a plant cell. Suggest **one** reason why he says this. (1 mark)

.................................................................................................................................................................

**5.** Complete the sentences below about the different parts of a cell by underlining the correct word in each of the boxes. (3 marks)

**(a)** Most of the chemical reactions in a cell take place in the

| cell membrane. |
| cytoplasm. |
| vacuole. |

**(b)** Energy from respiration is released in the

| cytoplasm. |
| cell wall. |
| mitochondria. |

**(c)** Proteins are synthesised at the

| chloroplasts. |
| ribosomes. |
| mitochondria. |

**6.** The diagram below shows a single-celled organism called an amoeba.

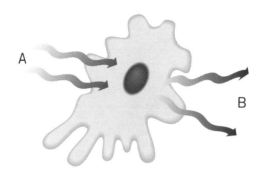

Substances pass in and out of the amoeba by diffusion.

**(a)** Suggest **two** substances that could be represented by arrows A.          (2 marks)

_____ and _____

**(b)** Suggest **two** substances that could be represented by arrows B.          (2 marks)

_____ and _____

**7.** Some students set up an experiment to investigate diffusion. They made a model cell using an artificial membrane that allowed small molecules such as water and glucose to pass through. They filled the cell with pure water and placed it in a solution containing glucose. They measured the concentration of glucose inside the cell every 20 minutes.

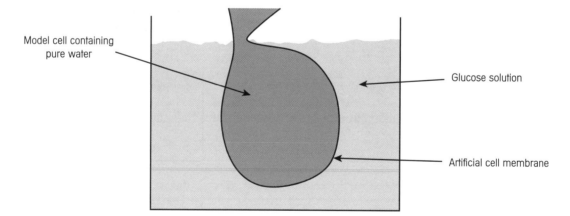

Model cell containing pure water

Glucose solution

Artificial cell membrane

Their results are shown on the graph below.

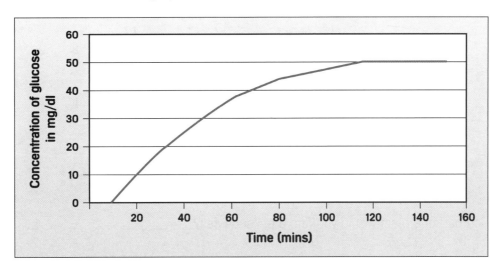

**(a)** What was the concentration of glucose inside the cell after 40 minutes?     (1 mark)

........................................................................................................................

**(b)** Describe what the graph is showing.     (2 marks)

........................................................................................................................

........................................................................................................................

**(c)** Explain what is happening.     (3 marks)

........................................................................................................................

........................................................................................................................

........................................................................................................................

**(d)** Why does the process appear to stop after 120 minutes?     (1 mark)

........................................................................................................................

........................................................................................................................

**8.** Complete the sentences below about diffusion by inserting the correct words.     (4 marks)

Diffusion is the spreading of ............................................. or any substances in a solution from an area

of ............................. concentration to an area of ............................. concentration.

The greater the difference in concentration, the ............................. the rate of diffusion.

**9.** The diagram shows a palisade cell.

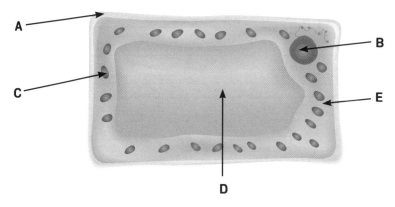

**(a)** In which part of a plant would you find a palisade cell? (1 mark)

.................................................................................................................................

**(b)** Which structures **(A–E)** match the following descriptions? Write the correct letter in each box. You may use the same letter more than once. (8 marks)

Where most chemical reactions take place ☐

Made of cellulose ☐

Contains chlorophyll ☐

Controls what the cell does ☐

Gives the cell rigidity and strength ☐

Filled with cell sap ☐

Where photosynthesis occurs ☐

Contains chromosomes ☐

**10.** The sentences below are about bacterial cells. Circle the correct words from each pair. (4 marks)

A bacterial cell consists of **cytoplasm / cytotoxin** surrounded by a cell membrane.

Outside the cell membrane is a **cell wall / guard cell**.

The cell walls in bacteria and plants are made of **the same substance / different substances**.

The genetic material in bacteria is found **in a nucleus / free within the cell**.

**(Total: .............. / 41 marks)**

**1.** The diagram below shows the human digestive system

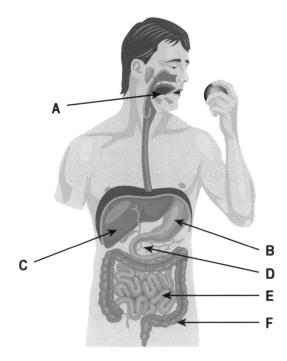

**(a)** Name the parts labelled A to F. (6 marks)

A ......................................................    B ......................................................

C ......................................................    D ......................................................

E ......................................................    F ......................................................

**(b)** Write the letter of the organ that produces bile. (1 mark)

.................................................................................................................................................................

**(c)** The pancreas is a gland and produces the hormone insulin. Name **one** other substance produced by the pancreas. (1 mark)

.................................................................................................................................................................

**2.** Complete the following passage by filling in the blanks, using some of the words below. (4 marks)

**gaps**      **epidermal**      **chloroplasts**      **phloem**

**water**      **mesophyll**      **gases**

Plants, like animals, have different tissues. ........................................................ tissue is found covering the

outer layers of the leaf. The ........................................ tissue carries out photosynthesis. The cells

of this tissue have ........................................ between them to allow easy passage

of ........................................ .

**3.** Read the following passage about burns and skin grafts.

> Patients with severe burns often require skin grafts. There are three options available.
>
> If the burn is not too severe, the burnt skin is removed and a thin layer of skin taken from an unburnt area of the patient is grafted on. Usually these grafts work well and the patient's own blood vessels quickly grow into the graft.
>
> If the patient has lost most of their skin through burns, scientists have developed a way of taking just a small piece of skin from the patient and growing this in the laboratory to form a layer of skin for grafting. The problem with these tissue-engineered sheets of skin is that growth of new blood vessels is slow, often leading to loss of the grafts.
>
> Another alternative for serious burns is artificial skin, which contains no living components. It is composed of silicon and collagen. This is not intended as a replacement skin, but is draped over the burn area and stimulates new skin to grow underneath it. Sometimes the new layer of skin is peeled off when the artificial layer is removed.

**(a)** Suggest **one** advantage of normal skin grafts. (1 mark)

........................................................................................................................................

**(b)** Why should slow growth of blood vessels in tissue-engineered sheets of skin lead to loss of grafts? (2 marks)

........................................................................................................................................

........................................................................................................................................

**(c)** Suggest **one** disadvantage of artificial skin grafts. (1 mark)

........................................................................................................................................

**(d)** What is the main difference between artificial skin and normal skin? (1 mark)

........................................................................................................................................

**(e)** The diagram shows part of a tissue-engineered sheet of skin cells.

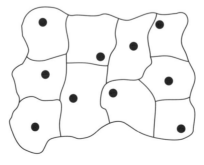

What is the name of these cells? (1 mark)

........................................................................................................................................

**4.** Organs are made up of a number of tissues. Match the type of tissue in **List A** with its function in **List B**. Draw a line to match each type with its function. (3 marks)

**List A**

| Glandular |
|---|

| Muscular |
|---|

| Nervous |
|---|

| Epithelial |
|---|

**List B**

| Can contract to bring about movement |
|---|

| A lining/covering tissue |
|---|

| Can carry electrical impulses |
|---|

| Can produce substances such as enzymes and hormones |
|---|

**5.** The picture below shows a plant.

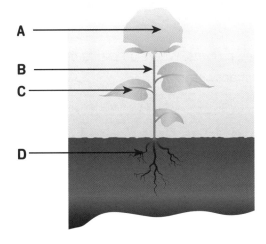

**(a)** Write the letter of the plant organ that is responsible for photosynthesis. (1 mark)

**(b)** Write the letter of the plant organ that is responsible for reproduction. (1 mark)

**(c)** What is the function of organ B? (1 mark)

(Total: .......... / 24 marks)

# B2 Photosynthesis

1. Complete the following equation for photosynthesis. (2 marks)

   carbon dioxide   +   ........................   ➞   glucose   +   ........................

2. **(a)** Apart from the ingredients given in the equation above, what **two** other factors are required for photosynthesis? (2 marks)

   **(i)** ........................................................................................................

   **(ii)** .......................................................................................................

   **(b) (i)** What is the name of the green pigment that absorbs the Sun's energy during photosynthesis? (1 mark)

   ................................................................................................................

   **(ii)** Where is this pigment found in the cell? (1 mark)

   ................................................................................................................

3. Where do plants obtain water required for photosynthesis? (1 mark)

   ................................................................................................................

4. Plants need nitrates to produce proteins. Where do plants obtain nitrates from?
   Tick the box next to the correct answer. (1 mark)

   From the soil ⬭

   From the leaves ⬭

   From oxygen ⬭

   From photosynthesis ⬭

5. Which of the following are factors that can limit the rate of photosynthesis?
   Tick the boxes next to the **three** correct options. (3 marks)

   Amount of oxygen ⬭

   Amount of light ⬭

   Amount of carbon dioxide ⬭

   Amount of chlorophyll ⬭

   Temperature ⬭

6. Circle the correct temperature option in the following sentence. (1 mark)

   The temperature at which enzymes controlling photosynthesis are destroyed is

   **14°C / 25°C / 32°C / 45°C**

**7.** Explain why too little light can have a negative effect on a plant. (2 marks)

........................................................................................................................................................

........................................................................................................................................................

**8.** A plant is receiving plenty of light but its rate of photosynthesis stops increasing. What other factors might be responsible? Tick the box next to the correct option. (1 mark)

Amount of carbon dioxide or the amount of oxygen ⬭

Amount of carbon dioxide or the temperature ⬭

Amount of chlorophyll or the temperature ⬭

Amount of glucose or the amount of oxygen ⬭

**9.** Fill in the missing words to complete the following sentence. (2 marks)

To control the rate of ................................................. greenhouses can be used to make plants

................................................. more quickly, becoming bigger and stronger.

**10.** Some students investigated the effect of temperature on the rate of photosynthesis in pondweed. They set up the equipment shown below and changed the temperature using ice and hot water. They counted the number of bubbles given off every minute at different temperatures.

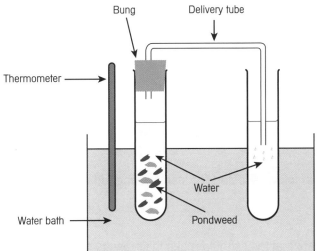

**(a)** Why did the students use a water bath? (1 mark)

........................................................................................................................................................

**(b)** What should the students have done to make the investigation fair? (1 mark)

........................................................................................................................................................

**(c)** How could the students make sure their results were reliable? (1 mark)

........................................................................................................................................................

**11.** Most of the carbon dioxide that a plant uses during photosynthesis is absorbed from the air.

Give **one** other source of carbon dioxide for a plant. Draw a circle around your answer.     (1 mark)

**the soil**          **respiration in the plant**          **osmosis in the plant**          **water**

**12.** Describe **two** uses of glucose in plants and algae.     (2 marks)

_____

_____

**13.** Glucose is difficult for plants to store.

**(a)** What is glucose changed into?     (1 mark)

_____

**(b)** Apart from stems, give **two** other places where plants store this substance.     (2 marks)

**(i)** _____

**(ii)** _____

**(c)** State the reaction that uses glucose in plants.     (1 mark)

_____

**14.** A group of students carried out a common experiment to prove that leaves carry out photosynthesis. They selected one plant from their classroom window and covered part of a single leaf in foil. The students then carried out experiments testing for the presence of starch using iodine, a yellowy brown liquid. A positive test will turn iodine blue/black.

**(a)** What is prevented from reaching the leaf by the foil?     (1 mark)

_____

**(b)** If the leaf covered in foil was tested for starch using iodine, what result would you expect? (1 mark)

_____

**(c)** One student suggests that they should make their results more reliable. What should they do? (1 mark)

_____

**(d)** Another student in the class says that they should have a control in their investigation. What would they use as the control?     (1 mark)

_____

**(Total: _____ / 31 marks)**

**1.** Temperature and availability of nutrients are two physical factors that affect the distribution of organisms. What other factors affect the distribution of organisms? Tick **three** options.     (3 marks)

Amount of carbon monoxide  ◯                Availability of water  ◯

Availability of oxygen and carbon dioxide  ◯       Amount of light  ◯

Availability of lichens  ◯                Availability of rocks  ◯

**2.** A class of students was asked to estimate the number of daisies on the school field. The field is 60m by 90m and has an area of $5400m^2$. They decided to use quadrats that were $1m^2$.

**(a)** Which is the best way of using quadrats in this investigation? Tick **one** option.     (1 mark)

Place all the quadrats where there are lots of plants.  ◯

Place all the quadrats randomly in the field.  ◯

Place all the quadrats where dandelions do not grow.  ◯

Each student collected data by using ten quadrats. The results of one student, Shaun, are shown in the table below.

| Quadrat | 1 | 2 | 3 | 4 | 5 | 6 | 7 | 8 | 9 | 10 |
|---|---|---|---|---|---|---|---|---|---|---|
| Number of daisies | 5 | 2 | 1 | 0 | 4 | 5 | 2 | 0 | 6 | 3 |

**(b)** Calculate the mean number of dandelions per quadrat counted by Shaun. Show clearly how you worked out your answer.     (2 marks)

_____

_____

**(c)** Another student, Bethany, calculated a mean of 2.3 daisies per quadrat from her results. Using Bethany's results, estimate the total number of daisies in the whole field by using the equation below. Show clearly how you work out your answer.     (2 marks)

| Estimated number of daisies on the field | = | Mean number of daisies per quadrat | × | Number of quadrats that would fit in the field |
|---|---|---|---|---|

_____

_____

Estimated number of daisies on the field _____

3. Duckweed is a small floating plant found in ponds. It reproduces quite quickly to produce large populations. Helen decided to investigate duckweed by growing some in a beaker of water. She counted the number of duckweed at regular intervals. Her results are shown in the table below.

| Day | 1 | 4 | 8 | 10 | 15 | 19 | 20 | 23 | 26 | 30 |
|---|---|---|---|---|---|---|---|---|---|---|
| **Number of plants** | 1 | 2 | 3 | 4 | 15 | 28 | 30 | 28 | 29 | 29 |

**(a)** Plot a graph of the results to show how the population changed over time. (2 marks)

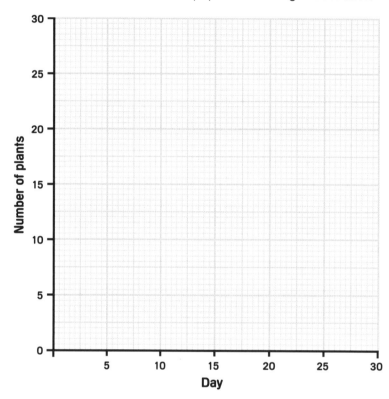

**(b)** Describe what is happening to the population between day one and day ten. (1 mark)

_____

**(c)** Suggest **two** factors that could have prevented the population from continuing to increase. (2 marks)

_____

_____

**(Total: ........... / 13 marks)**

1.   What are protein molecules made up of? Tick **one** option.            (1 mark)

Glucose molecules ☐

Starch molecules ☐

Amino acid molecules ☐

Glycerol and fatty acid molecules ☐

2.   Circle the correct options in the following sentences.

(a) An enzyme is a **biological / chemical** catalyst that **speeds up / slows down** the rate of reactions in an organism.                                                      (2 marks)

(b) Enzymes are made from **carbohydrate / fat / vitamin / protein** molecules. They are made up of long chains of **DNA / amino acids / fatty acids / starch** molecules.            (2 marks)

3.   Briefly explain what happens to an enzyme if the temperature goes too high.    (2 marks)

4.   (a) Name the organ in the body that produces bile.                       (1 mark)

(b) Where is bile stored in the human body?                              (1 mark)

(c) Into which part of the digestive system is bile released?            (1 mark)

(d) Why is it necessary for bile to neutralise the acid that was added to food in the stomach?                                                                      (1 mark)

5.   Amylase is a carbohydrase enzyme. List **three** places in the digestive system where it is produced.                                                            (3 marks)

(a) ..........................................................................................................................................................

(b) ..........................................................................................................................................................

(c) ..........................................................................................................................................................

# B2 | Proteins – their Functions and Uses

**6.** Different enzymes act on specific nutrients. Draw lines to match the correct enzyme to the nutrient it works on, then match the correct nutrient with its smaller sub-unit. **(3 marks)**

| Protease |
| --- |
| Amylase |
| Lipase |

| Fats |
| --- |
| Proteins |
| Carbohydrates |

| Amino acids |
| --- |
| Glycerol and fatty acids |
| Glucose |

**7.** Which of the following organs produce digestive enzymes? Tick **four** correct options. **(4 marks)**

Rectum ⬭

Large intestine ⬭

Salivary glands ⬭

Stomach ⬭

Gall bladder ⬭

Pancreas ⬭

Small intestine ⬭

Liver ⬭

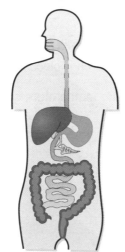

**8.** Enzymes are used in industry and in the home. Enzymes are often used in the manufacture of baby food to help pre-digest certain foods.

**(a)** When proteins are pre-digested in industry, what type of enzyme is used? **(1 mark)**

.............................................................................................................................................

**(b)** What will these enzymes produce? **(1 mark)**

.............................................................................................................................................

A baby food manufacturer wants to improve the efficiency of his business and use the enzyme that pre-digests the protein the fastest. He already uses enzyme X, which takes 15 minutes to completely pre-digest the protein.

He investigates four other enzymes; A, B, C and D. He uses the same concentration of enzyme as well as the same amount of protein for each experiment. The table below shows the time taken for the enzymes 'investigated' to completely pre-digest the protein.

| Enzyme | A | B | C | D |
| --- | --- | --- | --- | --- |
| Time taken to completely pre-digest protein (minutes) | 19 | 6 | 13 | 16 |

**(c)** What is the independent variable being tested? (1 mark)

**(d)** The manufacturer started plotting the results on the chart below. Complete the chart by plotting the remaining results. (4 marks)

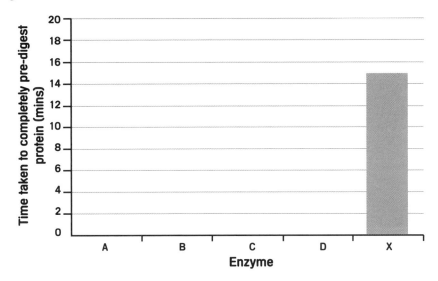

**(e)** Which enzyme would you recommend the manufacturer should use? Explain why. (2 marks)

**(f)** The research and development team at the company are not convinced by the results from this investigation. What could the manufacturer do to increase the reliability of their results? (1 mark)

**9.** Which **two** enzymes might biological detergents contain? Tick the **two** correct options. (2 marks)

Fat-digesting ☐

Glucose-digesting ☐

Bile-digesting ☐

Protein-digesting ☐

**10.** Match statements **A**, **B**, and **C** with the enzymes **1–3** listed below. Write the appropriate numbers in the boxes provided. (3 marks)

**1. Carbohydrases**      **2. Proteases**      **3. Isomerases**

**A** Used to produce fructose syrup used in slimming foods ☐

**B** Used to pre-digest protein in baby foods ☐

**C** Used to convert starch into sugar syrup ☐

**11.** Here are some of the properties of enzymes:

- They are easily broken down by high temperature or the wrong pH.

- They are soluble in water, so it may be difficult to separate them from products.

- They are expensive.

- They work well at 25–45°C.

- They all work at atmospheric pressures.

Use only the information above to answer the following questions.

**(a)** Give **two** advantages of using enzymes in industry.           (2 marks)

   **(i)** ..............................................................................................................................................................

   **(ii)** .............................................................................................................................................................

**(b)** Give **two** disadvantages of using enzymes in industry.           (2 marks)

   **(i)** ..............................................................................................................................................................

   **(ii)** .............................................................................................................................................................

**12.** *In this question you will be assessed on using good English, organising information and using specialist terms where appropriate.*

Fructose syrup is much sweeter than glucose syrup. Explain why manufacturers of slimming foods use fructose syrup rather than glucose syrup.           (4 marks)

..................................................................................................................................................................

..................................................................................................................................................................

..................................................................................................................................................................

..................................................................................................................................................................

..................................................................................................................................................................

Yogurt Drink
IDEAL FOR
WEIGHT LOSS

Contains
fructose
sugar

**(Total: ............ / 44 marks)**

**1.** List **three** things that the energy produced in aerobic respiration is used for. (3 marks)

**(a)** ................................................................................................

**(b)** ................................................................................................

**(c)** ................................................................................................

**2.** What is aerobic respiration? Tick the correct option. (1 mark)

Respiration in the absence of oxygen ⬭

Respiration in the presence of oxygen ⬭

Respiration that produces lactic acid ⬭

Respiration that uses carbon dioxide ⬭

**3.** Describe when aerobic respiration occurs. (1 mark)

................................................................................................

**4.** Fill in the missing gaps to complete the word equation for aerobic respiration. (1 mark)

glucose + ............................... ➞ ............................... + water + energy

**5.** Fill in the missing words to complete the following sentences. (2 marks)

**(a)** Energy from respiration is used to enable muscles to ............................... .

**(b)** Aerobic respiration is a very ............................... way of producing energy.

**6.** How do glucose and oxygen get to the respiring cells? (1 mark)

................................................................................................

**7.** Name where most of the reactions involved in aerobic respiration take place. (1 mark)

................................................................................................

**8.** List **three** ways in which the water produced in aerobic respiration is lost from the body. (3 marks)

**(a)** ................................................................................................

**(b)** ................................................................................................

**(c)** ................................................................................................

**9.** What is anaerobic respiration? Tick the correct option. (1 mark)

Respiration in the absence of oxygen ⬭

Respiration in the presence of oxygen ⬭

Respiration that uses lactic acid ⬭

Respiration that uses carbon dioxide ⬭

**10.** Circle the correct option in the following sentence. (1 mark)

If our muscles are subjected to long periods of **light / vigorous / slow** activity, they become fatigued.

**11.** What is the waste product of anaerobic respiration? Tick the correct option. (1 mark)

Hydrochloric acid ⬭

Sulfuric acid ⬭

Lactic acid ⬭

Aerobic respiration ⬭

**12.** Are these sentences **true** or **false**? Circle the correct option. (3 marks)

**(a)** Lactic acid makes the muscles feel tired and rubbery. True / False

**(b)** Anaerobic respiration produces a small amount of energy quickly. True / False

**(c)** Anaerobic respiration is more efficient than aerobic respiration. True / False

**13.** List **three** differences between aerobic and anaerobic respiration. (3 marks)

**(a)** ......................................................................................................................................

**(b)** ......................................................................................................................................

**(c)** ......................................................................................................................................

**14.** Circle the correct options in the following paragraph. (5 marks)

When you exercise your heart rate **decreases / increases**, which causes the flow of blood to your muscles to **decrease / increase**. When you exercise your breathing rate also **increases / decreases** to speed up the removal of **carbon dioxide / oxygen** from your muscles and the transport of **carbon dioxide / oxygen** to your muscles.

**15.** Fill in the missing words to complete the following sentences. (3 marks)

During exercise, the supply of oxygen and ............................................. is ............................................. .

This speeds up the removal of ............................................. .

**16.** Two students wanted to find out who was the fittest. They carried out a simple investigation where they did star jumps for three minutes. They recorded their pulse rate before the activity and every minute afterwards. Their results are given in the table below.

| Time (mins) | Pulse rate (beats/min) | |
| --- | --- | --- |
| | Student A | Student B |
| Before activity | 68 | 72 |
| 1 minute after | 116 | 160 |
| 2 minutes after | 120 | 175 |
| 3 minutes after | 116 | 168 |
| 4 minutes after | 72 | 148 |
| 5 minutes after | 66 | 92 |
| 6 minutes after | 68 | 76 |

The results for student A have been plotted on the graph below.

**(a)** Add the data from Student B's column to the graph                                    (1 mark)

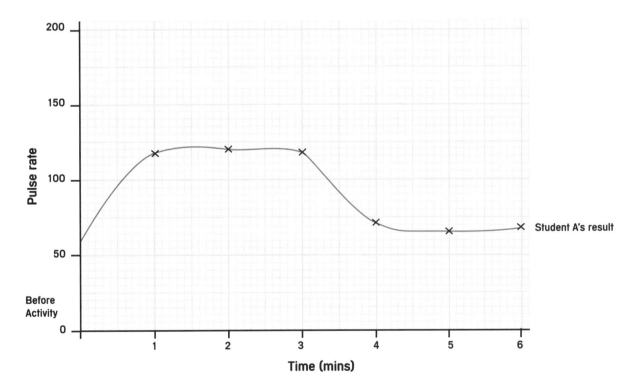

**(b)** Suggest which student was fitter. Draw a ring around your answer.                     (1 mark)

**Student A  /  Student B**

**(c)** Give **two** reasons for your answer.                                               (2 marks)

**(i)** ........................................................................................................................................

**(ii)** ........................................................................................................................................

**(d)** Explain why the pulse rate in both students increased. Give **two** reasons. (2 marks)

...........................................................................................................................................

...........................................................................................................................................

**(e)** Both students experienced fatigue in their muscles. What substance caused the fatigue? (1 mark)

...........................................................................................................................................

**17.** Shaun wanted to prove that beetles carried out respiration. He filled two boiling tubes, A and B, with $2cm^3$ of limewater. In boiling tube A he rested a live beetle on a piece of gauze halfway up the tube (the beetle was not touching the limewater). Tube B contained only limewater. Both boiling tubes were sealed with a bung.

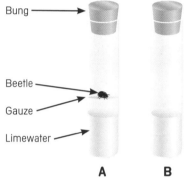

**(a)** What gas is limewater used to test for? (1 mark)

...........................................................................................................................................

**(b)** What would you expect to happen to the limewater in tube A? (1 mark)

...........................................................................................................................................

**(c)** Why did Shaun set up tube B? (1 mark)

...........................................................................................................................................

**(d)** How could Shaun increase the reliability of his results? (1 mark)

...........................................................................................................................................

**(e)** Shaun's friend said that he was cruel to use live animals in an experiment. Is Shaun right to carry out such experiments? Explain your answer. (1 mark)

...........................................................................................................................................

**(Total:** ............ **/ 44 marks)**

**Higher Tier**

**18.** Fill in the missing words to complete the following sentences.                    (3 marks)

**(a)** Anaerobic respiration occurs when the lungs and bloodstream cannot deliver enough

........................................ to the cells.

**(b)** When lactic acid builds up in the tissues, the muscles become ................................ .

**(c)** The amount of oxygen needed to break down the lactic acid in tissues is called

the ........................................ ........................................ .

**19.** Is more energy produced during aerobic respiration or anaerobic respiration?       (1 mark)

........................................................................................................

**20.** A sports scientist investigated the amount of lactic acid produced in the leg muscle of a short-distance runner. His results are given in the table below.

| Time (minutes) | 0 | 10 | 20 | 30 | 40 | 50 | 60 | 70 | 80 | 90 |
|---|---|---|---|---|---|---|---|---|---|---|
| Lactic acid (arbitrary units) | 0 | 1 | 6 | 13 | 8 | 6 | 4 | 3 | 1 | 0 |

**(a)** When did the level of lactic acid reach a maximum?                               (1 mark)

........................................................................................................

**(b)** How long does it take for the lactic acid to be removed from the muscle?          (2 marks)

........................................................................................................

**(c)** The lactic acid of a second athlete is investigated in the same way. Why is it important to keep variables the same in an investigation?                                        (1 mark)

........................................................................................................

**(d)** It takes 20 minutes for the level of lactic acid in the second athlete's muscles to return to normal. Which athlete is the fittest?                                              (1 mark)

........................................................................................................

**(e)** What gas is needed to break down the lactic acid?                                (1 mark)

........................................................................................................

(Total: ............ / 10 marks)

1. How many chromosomes does a human body cell contain? (1 mark)

2. What are the sex cells known as? Tick the correct option. (1 mark)

   Genes ◯

   Alleles ◯

   Gametes ◯

   Chromosomes ◯

3. What do the sex cells contain? Tick the correct option. (1 mark)

   Half the number of chromosomes as a normal body cell ◯

   The same number of chromosomes as a normal body cell ◯

   Twice the number of chromosomes as a normal body cell ◯

   Half the number of chromosomes of a sperm cell ◯

4. What is produced from the fusion of two sex cells? (1 mark)

5. **(a)** Circle the correct pair of sex chromosomes from the following options. (1 mark)

   **XY and YY**    **XX and XY**    **XX and YY**    **XF and XM**

   **(b)** Which of the following are the female sex chromosomes, and which are the male sex chromosomes. Label them correctly. (1 mark)

   **(i)** ............................................    **(ii)** ............................................

6. **(a)** Explain what determines the sex of an individual. (1 mark)

   **(b)** What is the likelihood of having a baby boy? (1 mark)

**7.** Mitosis is the division of body cells to make new cells.

**(a)** When is mitosis not used in dividing cells? Tick the correct option.   (1 mark)

Asexual reproduction ⬭          Gamete production ⬭

Repair ⬭          Growth ⬭

**(b)** Fill in the missing words to complete the following sentences.   (3 marks)

A copy of each ............................... is made before a cell divides. The new cell has the

same ............................... information as the ............................... cell.

**(c)** Circle the correct option in the following sentence.   (1 mark)

When one cell has undergone mitosis **1 / 2 / 4 / 8** 'daughter' cells will be made.

**8.** **(a)** Fill in the missing words to complete the following sentence.   (3 marks)

Meiosis takes place in the ............................... and testes, and produces

............................... and sperm containing 23 ................................

**(b)** What type of cells are produced in meiosis?   (1 mark)

..........................................................................................................

**9.** During human fertilisation the male and female sex cells join.

**(a)** How many chromosomes will the resulting cell contain?   (1 mark)

..........................................................................................................

**(b)** Describe what happens to the new cell.   (1 mark)

..........................................................................................................

**10.** **(a)** In which **two** places would you find stem cells?   (2 marks)

**(i)** ....................................................................................................

**(ii)** ...................................................................................................

**(b)** Explain why stem cells can be used to treat conditions such as paralysis.   (2 marks)

..........................................................................................................

..........................................................................................................

**(c)** Give **two** disadvantages of using stem cells.   (2 marks)

**(i)** ....................................................................................................

**(ii)** ...................................................................................................

**11.** How many alleles does the gene controlling tongue-rolling ability have? Tick the correct option. (1 mark)

One ◯

Two ◯

Three ◯

Four ◯

**12.** Fill in the missing words to complete the following sentences. (2 marks)

Where there are different alleles for a gene, the more powerful one is known as the

_____ allele and the weaker one is known as the _____ allele.

**13.** What does a genetic cross diagram show? (1 mark)

_____

**14.** **(a)** John has blue eyes. Both his parents have brown eyes. His mother's alleles are Bb.
   **(i)** What must John's father's alleles be? Tick the correct option. (1 mark)

   Bb ◯

   BB ◯

   bb ◯

   BBb ◯

   **(ii)** What alleles does John have? _____ (1 mark)

   **(b)** Circle the correct option in the following sentence. (1 mark)

   If both parents have blue eyes there is a **0% / 24% / 50% / 100%** chance that they will have a child with brown eyes.

**15.** Fill in the missing words to complete the following sentences.

   **(a)** A _____ allele will control the characteristics of a gene if it is present on only one chromosome, or if it is present on both chromosomes. (1 mark)

   **(b)** A _____ allele will only control the characteristic of a gene if it is present on both chromosomes. (1 mark)

**16.** What do the two strands of a DNA molecule coil together to form? Tick the correct box. **(1 mark)**

Double spring ⬭   Double spiral ⬭

Double twist ⬭   Double helix ⬭

**17.** Fill in the missing words to complete the following sentences. **(4 marks)**

**(a)** Polydactyly is a disorder that causes extra fingers or toes. It's caused by a ........................

allele. Only ........................ parent needs to have the disorder.

**(b)** Cystic fibrosis is caused by a ........................ allele. It must be inherited from both

parents. The parents might not have the disorder, but they might be ........................ .

**18.** The diagram below shows the inheritance of cystic fibrosis in a family.

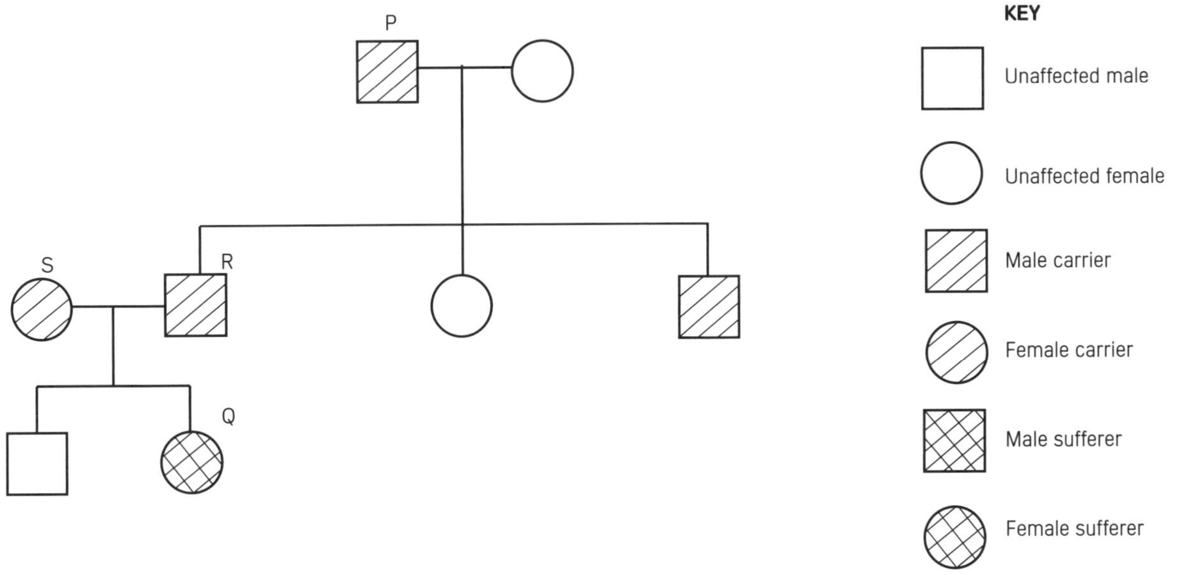

**KEY**

☐ Unaffected male

◯ Unaffected female

▨ Male carrier

◯ Female carrier

▨ Male sufferer

◯ Female sufferer

Cystic fibrosis is caused by a recessive allele, f. The dominant allele of the gene is represented by F.

**(a)** Give the alleles for person P ........................ . **(1 mark)**

**(b)** Give the alleles for person Q ........................ **(1 mark)**

**19.** Choose the correct words from the options given to complete the following sentence. **(3 marks)**

**structure**      **function**      **cells**

Differentiation is the result of ........................ developing a specialised

........................ to carry out a specific ........................ .

**(Total: ........ / 44 marks)**

**20.** Using the correct genetic terms, describe the following alleles. (3 marks)

**(a)** BB ........................................................................................................................

**(b)** Bb ........................................................................................................................

**(c)** bb ........................................................................................................................

**21.** Match definitions **A**, **B**, **C** and **D** with the keywords **1–4** listed below. Write the appropriate numbers in the boxes provided. (4 marks)

**1. Dominant**        **2. Phenotype**

**3. Heterozygous**    **4. Homozygous**

**A**  What the organism looks like ☐     **B**  The stronger allele ☐

**C**  Both alleles are the same ☐     **D**  Different alleles ☐

**22.** **(a)** Complete this genetic diagram to show the possible genotypes of the offspring. (2 marks)

**(b)** Complete the following sentence. (1 mark)

There is a ................................... % chance that the offspring will have brown eyes.

**23.** How do genes code for a particular characteristic? (1 mark)

........................................................................................................................

........................................................................................................................

**24.** Rita likes to grow plants. One particular plant she grows can either have red flowers (homozygous dominant) or white flowers (homozygous recessive). She decides to cross the pollen from the red plant with ovum from the white.

Complete the genetic cross diagram below using R to represent the dominant allele and r for the recessive allele. (4 marks)

White flower (rr)

|  |  | Genotype of ovum (r) | Genotype of ovum (r) |
|---|---|---|---|
| Red flower (RR) | Genotype of pollen (R) | (a) | (b) |
|  | Genotype of pollen (R) | (c) | (d) |

**25.** Complete the following sentences by circling the correct words in bold. (5 marks)

**(a)** A pea plant with a tall **genotype / phenotype** could have a **genotype / phenotype** TT or Tt.

**(b)** A tall pea plant with the genotype TT is **homozygous / heterozygous** dominant.

**(c)** A tall pea plant with genotype Tt is **homozygous / heterozygous**.

**(d)** A dwarf pea plant with genotype tt is **homozygous / heterozygous** recessive.

**26.** Explain in detail why it is possible for a couple to have four children, all daughters. (3 marks)

**27.** History relates how King Henry VIII was so desperate to have a male heir that he divorced or disposed of those of his wives who were unable to produce a son.

**(a)** What sex chromosomes are found in eggs? (1 mark)

**(b)** What sex chromosomes are found in sperm? (1 mark)

**(c)** Is it the father's or mother's gametes that determines the sex of an offspring? Explain your answer. (2 marks)

**28.** There are two types of wings on flies, short or normal. Using the symbol N to represent normal wing, and n for short wing, answer the following questions.

**(a) (i)** What is the phenotype for a fly that has the homozygous recessive genotype?    (1 mark)

.....................................................................................................................................................................

**(ii)** Circle the combination that represents homozygous recessive.    (1 mark)

**NN     nn     Nn**

**(b)** A heterozygous male fly mates with a homozygous recessive female. Complete the following genetic cross diagram.    (3 marks)

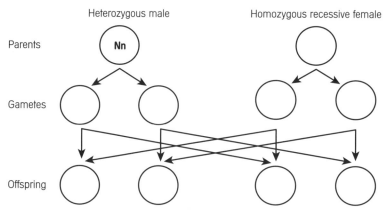

**(c)** What is the percentage chance of the parents having a short-winged offspring?    (1 mark)

.....................................................................................................................................................................

**(Total: ............... / 33 marks)**

**1.** Which of the following provides evidence for evolution? Tick the correct option. (1 mark)

Animals ☐          Fossils ☐

Plants ☐          Viruses ☐

**2.** Describe **one** way in which fossils are formed. (1 mark)

_____

_____

**3.** Explain why fossils can be quite hard to find. (1 mark)

_____

_____

**4.** **(a)** Explain what 'extinction' means. (1 mark)

_____

**(b)** Give **three** factors that could contribute to the extinction of a species. (3 marks)

**(i)** _____  **(ii)** _____  **(iii)** _____

**(c)** Give an example of a species that is now extinct. (1 mark)

_____

**(Total:** _____ **/ 8 marks)**

---

**Higher Tier**

**5.** New species can arise in a number of ways. Select the **four** correct options. (4 marks)

Isolation ☐                    Asexual reproduction ☐

Genetic variation ☐           Natural selection ☐

Taking cuttings ☐             Speciation ☐

**(Total:** _____ **/ 4 marks)**

**1.** **(a)** Complete this table. (9 marks)

| Atomic particle | Relative mass | Relative charge | Where is it found? |
|---|---|---|---|
| Proton | (i) | (ii) | (iii) |
| (iv) | (v) | (vi) | In shells |
| Neutron | (vii) | (viii) | (ix) |

**(b)** Briefly describe the structure of an atom in terms of the particles included in the table in **(a)**. (2 marks)

........................................................................................................................................

........................................................................................................................................

........................................................................................................................................

**(c)** The particles included in the table in **(a)** have relative charges. Why do atoms of a particular element have no overall charge? (1 mark)

........................................................................................................................................

........................................................................................................................................

**2.** The atomic number of sulfur is 16.

**(a)** What does the atomic number tell us? (1 mark)

........................................................................................................................................

**(b)** The electronic configuration of sulfur is 2,8,6. What do these numbers tell us? (1 mark)

........................................................................................................................................

........................................................................................................................................

**(c)** What is the electronic configuration of aluminium? (1 mark)

........................................................................................................................................

**3.** Complete the diagrams by drawing the full electron configurations for these elements and write the electronic configuration next to the element.

**(a)** Hydrogen  .................... **(b)** Helium  .................... **(c)** Lithium (3 marks)

**(d)** Beryllium  .................... **(e)** Boron  .................... **(f)** Carbon (3 marks)

**(g)** Nitrogen  .................... **(h)** Oxygen  .................... **(i)** Fluorine (3 marks)

**(j)** Neon  .................... **(k)** Sodium  .................... **(l)** Magnesium (3 marks)

**(m)** Aluminium  .................... **(n)** Silicon  .................... **(o)** Phosphorus (3 marks)

**(p)** Sulfur  .................... **(q)** Chlorine  .................... **(r)** Argon (3 marks)

**(s)** Potassium **(t)** Calcium (2 marks)

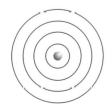

**4.** Lithium reacts with oxygen to produce lithium oxide. The symbol equation for this reaction is

$$4Li + O_2 \longrightarrow 2Li_2O$$

**(a)** Use the Periodic Table to find the atomic numbers for:

**(i)** Lithium _____ **(ii)** Oxygen _____ . (2 marks)

**(b)** Draw the electron configuration diagrams for a lithium atom and an oxygen atom.　　(2 marks)

**(i) Lithium**　　　**(ii) Oxygen**

 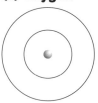

**(c)** Lithium oxide is an ionic compound. Use the diagrams that you drew in **(b)** to explain how:

**(i)** a lithium atom becomes a lithium ion.　　　　　　　　　　　　　　(1 mark)

_____

**(ii)** an oxygen atom becomes an oxide ion.　　　　　　　　　　　　　(1 mark)

_____

**(d)** Now draw an electron configuration diagram of lithium oxide (Li$_2$O).　　(1 mark)



**(e)** Lithium also reacts with chlorine to form lithium chloride (LiCl).
Explain how the ionic bond is formed in this compound.　　　　　　(1 mark)

_____

**5.** What is a covalent bond?　　　　　　　　　　　　　　　　　　　　(2 marks)

_____

_____

**6.** The diagram represents a molecule of hydrogen chloride. It is a gas at room temperature.

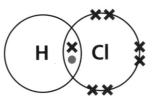

**(a)** What type of particles are represented by: (2 marks)

**(i)** The dot _____ **(ii)** The crosses _____

**(b)** Why is hydrogen chloride a gas at room temperature? (1 mark)

_____

**7.** Oxygen is a gas of molecules made up of two oxygen atoms and is represented by $O_2$. Oxygen atoms have six electrons in their outer shell.

**(a)** Draw two individual oxygen atoms in the box below. (2 marks)

**(b)** Draw a pair of oxygen atoms bonded together to form an $O_2$ molecule. (2 marks)

| (a) | (b) |
|---|---|
|  |  |

**(c)** What is the name of the bond that exists between the pair of atoms in **(b)**? (1 mark)

_____

**8.** Hydrogen atoms join together to form hydrogen molecules.

**(a)** What is the name of the bond that is formed between the atoms in a molecule of hydrogen? (1 mark)

_____

**(b)** A molecule of hydrogen can be represented by the following three diagrams:

**1** H—H

**2**

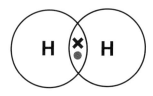

**3** H ⨯• H

Use the Periodic Table and this information to complete the table below by drawing the **three** structural representations for each substance.

| Substance | Formula | Structural formula | | | |
|-----------|---------|---|---|---|---|
| | | **1** | **2** | **3** | |
| Nitrogen | $N_2$ | | | | (3 marks) |
| Ammonia | $NH_3$ | | | | (3 marks) |
| Water | $H_2O$ | | | | (3 marks) |
| Bromine | $Br_2$ | | | | (3 marks) |
| Methane | $CH_4$ | | | | (3 marks) |
| Chlorine | $Cl_2$ | | | | (3 marks) |

**9.** **(a)** The diagrams below show the three forms of elemental carbon. Write the correct name for each form under its structure, in the boxes provided. (3 marks)

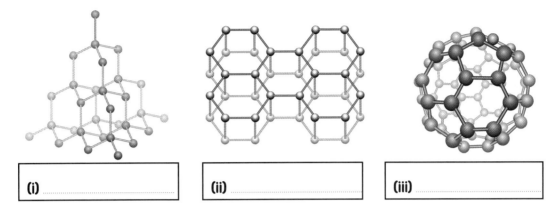

(i) ............................................

(ii) ............................................

(iii) ............................................

**(b)** Why does diamond have a very high melting point? (1 mark)

..........................................................................................................................

..........................................................................................................................

**(c)** Explain why graphite is an electrical conductor. (1 mark)

..........................................................................................................................

..........................................................................................................................

**(d)** Graphite can be used as a solid lubricant. Give a reason for this. (1 mark)

..........................................................................................................................

..........................................................................................................................

**10.** **(a)** Silica ($SiO_2$) is a pure form of sand. Why does silica have a high melting point? (1 mark)

..........................................................................................................................

..........................................................................................................................

**(b)** Describe how the atoms in silica are bonded to each other. (1 mark)

..........................................................................................................................

..........................................................................................................................

**11.** Nanoparticles are extremely small particles and are between 1 and 100 nanometres across.

**(a)** How many nanometres are there in 1mm? (1 mark)

**(b)** How can nanoparticles be used to make industrial catalysts? (1 mark)

**(c)** Briefly describe the new technology that has enabled scientists to see and control atoms at this small scale. (2 marks)

**(d)** Write down **two** ways in which nanoparticles have different properties from the same materials in bulk. (2 marks)

**12.** Nanocomposite materials have been developed for a variety of applications.

**(a)** In what way are nanocomposite polymers different to ordinary plastics? (2 marks)

**(b)** Write down **four** ways in which nanocomposite materials can be used. (4 marks)

**13.** Complete the table by writing down at least **two** uses for each example. The first box has been completed for you.

| Substance | What are its properties? | What can it be used for? | |
|---|---|---|---|
| Metal | Strong, shiny, good conductor of heat and electricity, malleable (can be bent easily). | Electrical wiring, saucepans, car body parts, jewellery | |
| Non-metal | Brittle, insulator. | (a) | (2 marks) |
| Polymer | Lightweight, flexible, waterproof. | (b) | (2 marks) |
| Ionic compound | Hard, crystalline, dissolves in water, high melting and boiling points, does not conduct when solid but conducts electricity when molten or dissolved. | (c) | (2 marks) |
| Molecular covalent | Soft, low melting point, does not conduct electricity. | (d) | (2 marks) |
| Macro-molecules | Hard and have a high melting point. | (e) | (2 marks) |
| Nanomaterial | Very strong and has a very big surface area, conducts electricity. | (f) | (2 marks) |

**(Total: ........... / 104 marks)**

1. **(a)** Label the following segment from the Periodic Table with the words **atomic number, mass number, chemical symbol** and **element name**. (4 marks)

```
┌─────────────────┐   ┌────────────────────────────┐
│        4        │   │                            │
│                 │   └────────────────────────────┘
│                 │   ┌────────────────────────────┐
│       He        │   │                            │
│     Helium      │   └────────────────────────────┘
│                 │   ┌────────────────────────────┐
│                 │   │                            │
│                 │   └────────────────────────────┘
│        2        │   ┌────────────────────────────┐
│                 │   │                            │
└─────────────────┘   └────────────────────────────┘
```

**(b)** What is the atomic number of helium? (1 mark)

**(c)** What is the mass number of helium? (1 mark)

**(d)** How many electrons does an atom of helium have? (1 mark)

**(e)** How many neutrons does an atom of helium have? (1 mark)

**(f)** Use the Periodic Table to find the name and symbol of the elements with these atomic numbers. (4 marks)

**(i)** 12

**(ii)** 8

**(iii)** 17

**(iv)** 22

**2.** Complete the following table. The first column has been done for you. (7 marks)

| | $^{12}_{6}C$ | $^{59}_{27}Co$ | $^{19}_{9}F$ | $^{24}_{12}Mg$ | $^{56}_{26}Fe$ | $^{16}_{8}O$ | $^{31}_{15}P$ | $^{40}_{18}Ar$ |
|---|---|---|---|---|---|---|---|---|
| **Number of protons** | 6 | | | | | | | |
| **Number of neutrons** | 6 | | | | | | | |
| **Number of electrons** | 6 | | | | | | | |
| **Element** | Carbon | | | | | | | |

**3.** What is an isotope? (1 mark)

.................................................................................................................................................

**4.** The following are symbol representations of two isotopes of carbon.

$$^{12}_{6}C \qquad\qquad ^{14}_{6}C$$

**(a)** How do we know that they are isotopes of carbon? (1 mark)

.................................................................................................................................................

**(b)** Complete the table below. (2 marks)

| | $^{12}_{6}C$ | $^{14}_{6}C$ |
|---|---|---|
| **Number of protons** | | |
| **Number of neutrons** | | |
| **Number of electrons** | | |

**5.** Use the Periodic Table to find out the relative atomic masses of the following elements: (9 marks)

**(a)** Sodium ....................     **(b)** Calcium ....................

**(c)** Copper ....................     **(d)** Oxygen ....................

**(e)** Hydrogen ....................     **(f)** Aluminium ....................

**(g)** Titanium ....................     **(h)** Bromine ....................

**(i)** Nitrogen ....................

**6.** Work out the relative formula masses of the following compounds: (6 marks)

**(a)** Water ($H_2O$) ....................

**(b)** Calcium carbonate ($CaCO_3$) ....................

**(c)** Iron oxide ($Fe_2O_3$) ....................

**(d)** Carbon dioxide ($CO_2$) ....................

**(e)** Calcium hydroxide ($Ca(OH)_2$) ....................

**(f)** Ammonium sulfate (($NH_4)_2SO_4$) ....................

**7.** **(a)** What is meant by the term 'atom economy'? (2 marks)

........................................................................................................

........................................................................................................

**(b)** What is the equation that is used to calculate the atom economy in a reaction? (2 marks)

........................................................................................................

**8.** Write down **three** reasons why it is not possible to obtain the full, calculated mass of a product from a reaction. (3 marks)

........................................................................................................

........................................................................................................

........................................................................................................

........................................................................................................

**9.** The equation for the main reaction to make ammonia is:

$$N_2 + 3H_2 \rightleftharpoons 2NH_3$$

**(a)** What does the symbol $\rightleftharpoons$ tell you about this reaction?   (1 mark)

**(b)** From where are the following raw materials obtained?   (2 marks)

**(i)** Nitrogen

**(ii)** Hydrogen

**(c)** What effect does increasing the temperature have on the rate and the yield of this process?   (1 mark)

**(Total: ......... / 49 marks)**

## Higher Tier

**10.** Write down the equation that relates the percentage amount of product obtained in a reaction to the maximum amount of product that could have been obtained in theory.   (2 marks)

**11.** Which is best, 0% yield or 100% yield? Give a reason why.   (2 marks)

**12.** In an experiment, James reacted solid magnesium oxide with sulfuric acid to make magnesium sulfate and water:

$$MgO(s) + H_2SO_4(aq) \longrightarrow MgSO_4(aq) + H_2O(l)$$

He used the apparatus shown below. First, he warmed the acid and magnesium oxide until they had fully reacted. Then he poured the solution into an evaporating basin and heated it until all the water had evaporated.

Heat          Heat

**(a)** List **two** ways in which James might have lost some of his product (the magnesium sulfate). (2 marks)

........................................................................................

........................................................................................

**(b)** What would this do to his percentage yield? (1 mark)

........................................................................................

**(c)** James predicted that he should make 24g of magnesium sulfate, but when he measured the mass of his solid product, there was only 18g. Work out his percentage yield. (1 mark)

........................................................................................

**(d)** Work out the missing values and fill in the gaps in the table below. (5 marks)

| Predicted yield | Actual yield | Percentage yield |
|---|---|---|
| 25g | 20g | **(i)** ............... |
| 80g | 70g | **(ii)** ............... |
| 1kg | 950g | **(iii)** ............... |
| 150g | **(iv)** ............... | 90% |
| **(v)** ............... | 130 kg | 65% |

**(Total:** ............ **/ 13 marks)**

1. Lee, Anita and Jane decided to investigate the rate of reaction between calcium carbonate and hydrochloric acid using marble chips.

The equation for the reaction is

$$CaCO_3(s) + 2HCl(aq) \longrightarrow CaCl_2(aq) + H_2O + CO_2(g)$$

calcium carbonate + hydrochloric acid ⟶ calcium chloride + water + carbon dioxide

They used the apparatus shown below:

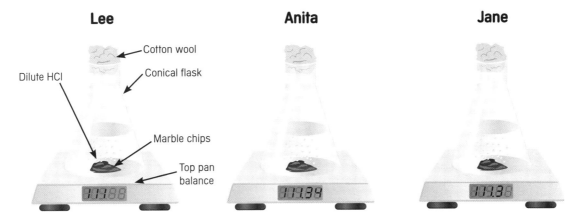

They obtained the following results:

| Time in minutes | Mass of flask and contents (g) | | |
|:---:|:---:|:---:|:---:|
| | Lee | Anita | Jane |
| 0 | 111 | 111.34 | 111.3 |
| 1 | 111 | 111.24 | 111.2 |
| 2 | 111 | 111.22 | 111.2 |
| 3 | 111 | 111.21 | 111.2 |
| 4 | 111 | 111.20 | 111.2 |
| 5 | 111 | 111.20 | 111.2 |
| 6 | 111 | 111.19 | 111.2 |
| 7 | 111 | 111.18 | 111.2 |
| 8 | 111 | 111.18 | 111.2 |
| 9 | 111 | 111.17 | 111.2 |
| 10 | 111 | 111.16 | 111.2 |

**(a)** Which student used the balance with the highest resolution? (1 mark)

.................................................................................................................................................

**(b)** Why should the balance used have a high resolution? (1 mark)

.................................................................................................................................................

**(c)** Plot the following on the graph paper below:

    **(i)**  Label the axes                                                                (1 mark)

    **(ii)** Plot Anita's results                                                     (1 mark)

    **(iii)** Complete the line of best fit                                           (1 mark)

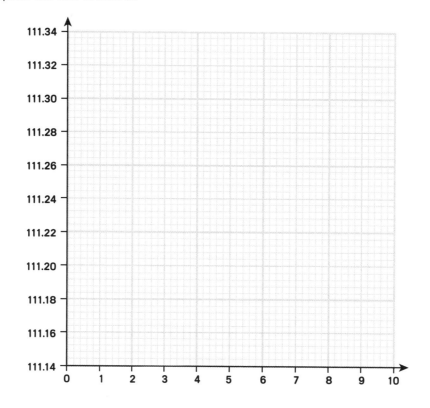

**(d)** Use the graph to find the mass of the flask and its contents after 1.5 minutes.     (2 marks)

 

**(e)** The mass of the flask and contents decreased during the experiment. Use the equation on page 49 to explain why.     (4 marks)

 

 

 

**(f)** The rate of reaction can be measured by the steepness of the graph line.

Describe how the rate of reaction changes with time in this experiment.     (2 marks)

# AQA GCSE Additional Science Workbook Answers

## Cells and Simple Cell Transport (pp 4–8)

1.

| Structure/ type of cell | Nucleus | Cytoplasm | Cell membrane | Cell wall |
|---|---|---|---|---|
| Plant cell | ✓ | ✓ | ✓ | ✓ |
| Bacterial cell | ✗ | ✓ | ✓ | ✓ |
| Animal cell | ✓ | ✓ | ✓ | ✗ |

   (*1 mark for each correct row*)
2. The cell has hair-like structures – To absorb water
   The cell is very large – To act as a food supply
   This cell has a tail – To swim
   This cell can be very long with branched endings – To carry nerve impulses
   (*1 correct = 1 mark; 2 correct = 2 marks; All 4 correct = 3 marks*)
3. **(a)** Red blood cell/Erythrocyte
   **(b)** It leaves more room for haemoglobin/more room to carry oxygen.
4. **(a)** It contains chloroplasts.
   **(b)** It does not have a cell wall.
5. **(a)** cytoplasm
   **(b)** mitochondria
   **(c)** ribosomes
6. **(a)** food; oxygen
   **(b)** carbon dioxide; waste products
7. **(a)** 25mg/dl
   **(b)** Between 0 and 120 minutes, the concentration of glucose inside the cell increases; Then it stops increasing.
   **(c)** Glucose is moving; From the glucose solution into the cell; By diffusion.
   **(d)** The concentration of glucose inside and outside the cell must be equal so there is no movement of glucose in either direction.
8. gases; high; low; faster.
9. **(a)** Leaf
   **(b)** E; A; C; B; A; D; C; B
10. cytoplasm; cell wall; different substances; free within the cell

## Tissues, Organs and Organ Systems (pp 9–11)

1. **(a)** A – salivary gland     B – stomach
   C – liver     D – pancreas
   E – small intestine     F – large intestine
   **(b)** C
   **(c) Any one from:** Enzymes; A named enzyme; Digestive juices.
2. Epidermal; mesophyll; gaps; gases
3. **(a) Any one from:** They work well; The patient's own blood vessels quickly grow into the graft.
   **(b)** The new tissue will not get sufficient oxygen and glucose if blood supply is poor; The tissue will then die.
   **(c) Any one from:** The new skin sometimes peels off when the artificial layer is removed; Artificial skin is not permanent.
   **(d)** Artificial skin contains no living components, normal skin is made of living cells.
   **(e)** Epithelial cells
4. Glandular – Can produce substances such as enzymes and hormones
   Muscular – Can contract to bring about movement
   Nervous – Can carry electrical impulses
   Epithelial – A lining/covering tissue
   (*1 correct = 1 mark; 2 correct = 2 marks; All 4 correct = 3 marks*)
5. **(a)** C
   **(b)** A
   **(c) Any one from:** Transport of nutrients; Transport of water (taken in by roots); Transport of sugar (made in the leaves).

## Photosynthesis (pp 12–14)

1. water; oxygen
2. **(a) (i–ii) In any order:** Sunlight; Chlorophyll.
   **(b) (i)** Chlorophyll
   **(ii)** Inside the chloroplasts in a leaf cell.
3. Through their roots from the soil.
4. From the soil.
5. Amount of light; Amount of carbon dioxide; Temperature.
6. 45°C
7. The rate of photosynthesis increases with light intensity; So the less sunlight there is, the lower the rate of photosynthesis will be.
8. Amount of carbon dioxide or the temperature.
9. photosynthesis; grow
10. **(a)** To keep the water temperature constant.
    **(b)** Keep all variables (except the one being investigated) the same, e.g. same amount of pondweed for each experiment, same amount of water for each experiment
    **(c)** Repeat their investigation.
11. respiration in the plant
12. **Any two from:** Used to produce fat or oil for storage; Used to produce cellulose, which strengthens the cell wall; Used to produce proteins; Used to make starch used in respiration
13. **(a) Any one from:** Starch; Oils/Fats
    **(b) (i-ii)** Roots; Leaves
    **(c)** Respiration
14. **(a)** Light
    **(b) Accept one from:** A negative result; No colour change.
    **(c)** Repeat their investigation.
    **(d)** A leaf that has not been covered up.

## Organisms and their Environment (pp 15–16)

1. Availability of water; Availability of oxygen and carbon dioxide; Amount of light
2. **(a)** Place all the quadrats randomly in the field.
   **(b)** (5 + 2 + 1 + 4 + 5 + 2 + 6 + 3) ÷ 10;
   = 28 ÷ 10 = 2.8
   **(c)** 2.3 × 5400; = 12 420
3. **(a)** (*1 mark for points correctly plotted; 1 mark for line drawn*)

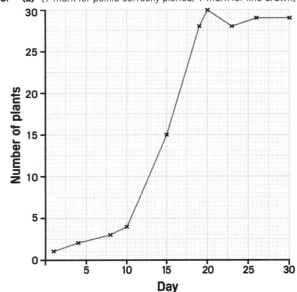

   **(b)** The population is slowly increasing.
   **(c) Any two from:** Competition for space; Competition for water; Competition for light; Lack of nutrients and accumulation of waste products; Disease or deficiency

## Proteins – their Functions and Uses (pp 17–20)

1. Amino acid molecules
2. **(a)** biological; speeds up
   **(b)** protein; amino acids
3. The enzyme's special shape will be destroyed; It will be unable to carry out its normal function.
4. **(a)** Liver
   **(b)** Gall bladder
   **(c)** Small intestine
   **(d)** It provides alkaline conditions in which enzymes in the small intestine work most effectively.
5. **(a–c) In any order:** Salivary glands; Pancreas; Small intestine.
6. Protease – Proteins – Amino acids; Amylase – Carbohydrates – Glucose; Lipase – Fats – Glycerol and fatty acids.
7. Salivary glands; Stomach; Pancreas; Small intestine
8. **(a)** Protease
   **(b)** Amino acids
   **(c)** Type of enzyme
   **(d)** (*Correctly plotted bar chart – 1 mark for each bar*)

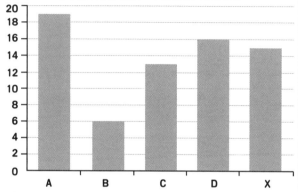

   **(e)** B; Because it is the quickest to completely pre-digest the protein.
   **(f)** Repeat the experiment several times.
9. Fat-digesting; Protein-digesting
10. A 3; B 2; C 1
11. **(a) (i–ii)** They work well at 25–45°C; They all work at atmospheric pressures.
    **(b) (i–ii) Any two from:** They are easily broken down by high temperature or the wrong pH; They are soluble in water, so it may be difficult to separate them from products; They are expensive.
12. **This is a model answer that would score full marks** As fructose is sweeter it can be used in smaller quantities, which makes it more cost-effective for the manufacturer. It also means that a person consuming the product will be taking in fewer calories, which will help in weight loss.

## Aerobic and Anaerobic Respiration (pp 21–25)

1. **(a–c)** Muscle contraction; Metabolism; Maintaining temperature; Building larger molecules from smaller ones
2. Respiration in the presence of oxygen
3. During normal everyday activities.
4. oxygen; carbon dioxide
5. **(a)** contract
   **(b)** efficient
6. By the bloodstream.
7. In the mitochondria in the cytoplasm in cells
8. **(a–c) Any three from:** As sweat; In moist breath; In urine; In faeces
9. Respiration in the absence of oxygen
10. vigorous
11. Lactic acid
12. **(a)** True
    **(b)** True
    **(c)** False
13. **(a–c) Any three from:** Oxygen used in aerobic respiration; More energy from aerobic; Carbon dioxide and water end products of aerobic; Lactic acid end product of anaerobic.
14. increases; increase; increases; carbon dioxide; oxygen
15. glucose; increased; carbon dioxide

16. **(a)**

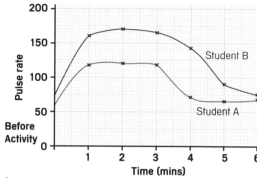

(*1 mark for points correctly plotted; 1 mark for line drawn; 1 mark for line labelled*)
   **(b)** Student A
   **(c) (i–ii)** Lower pulse rate increase; Quicker recovery time.
   **(d) Any two from:** To get more oxygen to the muscles; To get more glucose to the muscles; Faster removal of carbon dioxide; Faster removal of lactic acid.
   **(e)** Lactic acid
17. **(a)** Carbon dioxide
    **(b)** Turn cloudy
    **(c)** As a control
    **(d)** Carry out repeats using other beetles.
    **(e) Any sensible answer,** e.g. helps to develop knowledge; Beetle not harmed
18. **(a)** oxygen
    **(b)** fatigued/rubbery
    **(c)** oxygen debt
19. Aerobic respiration
20. **(a)** 30 minutes
    **(b)** 90 − 30 = 60 minutes
    (*1 for calculation, 1 for answer*)
    **(c)** It allows results to be fairly compared.
    **(d)** The second athlete
    **(e)** Oxygen

## Cell Division and Inheritance (pp 26–32)

1. 46/23 pairs
2. Gametes
3. Half the number of chromosomes as a normal body cell
4. A zygote
5. **(a)** XX and XY
   **(b) (i)** female
   **(ii)** male
6. **(a)** Whether the ovum is fertilised by an X-carrying sperm or a Y-carrying sperm.
   **(b)** 50%/half
7. **(a)** Gamete production
   **(b)** chromosome; genetic; parent
   **(c)** 2
8. **(a)** ovaries; eggs; chromosomes
   **(b)** Gametes
9. **(a)** 46
   **(b)** It divides repeatedly by mitosis to form a new individual.
10. **(a) (i–ii)** Human embryos; Adult bone marrow.
    **(b)** Stem cells can be made to differentiate into any type of cell; Including nerve cells and muscle cells.
    **(c) (i–ii) Any two from:** Expensive; High chance of rejection; Dependency on immunosuppressant drugs; Uncontrollable cell growth could cause cancer.
11. Two
12. dominant; recessive
13. Inheritance of genes.
14. **(a) (i)** Bb
    **(ii)** bb
    **(b)** 0%
15. **(a)** dominant
    **(b)** recessive
16. Double helix
17. **(a)** dominant; one
    **(b)** recessive; carriers
18. **(a)** Ff
    **(b)** ff

19. cells; structure; function
20. (a) BB = Homozygous dominant
    (b) Bb = Heterozygous
    (c) bb = Homozygous recessive
21. A 2; B 1; C 4; D 3
22. (a) Gametes: B; B; b; b (*1 mark*)
       Offspring: Bb; Bb; Bb; Bb (*1 mark*)
    (b) 100
23. By providing a code for a combination of amino acids that make up a protein.
24.

White flower (rr)

| | | Genotype of ovum (r) | Genotype of ovum (r) |
|---|---|---|---|
| Red flower (RR) | Genotype of pollen (R) | (a) Rr | (b) Rr |
| | Genotype of pollen (R) | (c) Rr | (d) Rr |

25. (a) phenotype; genotype
    (b) homozygous
    (c) heterozygous
    (d) homozygous
26. Sex is controlled by sex chromosomes – XX in females, XY in males; There is a 50% chance of an offspring being a boy or girl; in order to produce females the sperm need to carry the X chromosome and not the Y chromosome.
27. (a) X
    (b) X or Y
    (c) Father's; Because the male chromosome can be X or Y, mother's egg can only give X chromosome.
28. (a) (i) short wing
       (ii) nn
    (b) Parents (female): nn (*1 mark*); Gametes (male): N, n; (female): n, n (*1 mark*); Offspring (male): Nn, nn; (female) Nn, nn (*1 mark*)
    (c) 50%

## Speciation (p 33)

1. Fossils
2. **Any one from:** From parts of organisms that have not decayed; When parts of the organism are replaced by other materials as they decay; As preserved traces of organisms, e.g. footprints; trapped in resin, e.g. amber
3. **Any one from:** Many early forms of life were soft-bodied, which means they left few traces behind; Many fossils are destroyed by geological activity; Many fossils are hidden in layers of rock that are not accessible; Most animals rot and do not fossilize
4. (a) When all individuals of a kind (species) have died.
   (b) (i–iii) **Any three from:** New/increased competition; Change in environment; New predators; New disease; Single catastrophic event; Loss of habitat
   (c) Accept named extinct animal, e.g. dodo, species of dinosaur
5. Isolation; Genetic variation; Natural selection; Speciation.

## The Structure of Substances (pp 34–41)

1. (a) (i) 1
       (ii) +1
       (iii) Nucleus
       (iv) Electron
       (v) 0.0005
       (vi) −1
       (vii) 1
       (viii) 0
       (ix) Nucleus
   (b) Protons and neutrons present in the nucleus; with the electrons orbiting around them in shells.
   (c) There is an equal number of oppositely charged protons and electrons.
2. (a) The number of protons in one atom of the element.
   (b) That the first shell contains 2 electrons, 8 electrons in the second shell and 6 electrons in the third (outer) shell.
   (c) 2, 8, 3

3.

| (a) Hydrogen, H | (b) Helium, He | (c) Lithium, Li | (d) Beryllium, Be | (e) Boron, B | (f) Carbon, C |
|---|---|---|---|---|---|
| 1 | 2 | 2,1 | 2,2 | 2,3 | 2,4 |
| (g) Nitrogen, N | (h) Oxygen, O | (i) Fluorine, F | (j) Neon, Ne | (k) Sodium, Na | (l) Magnesium, Mg |
| 2,5 | 2,6 | 2,7 | 2,8 | 2,8,1 | 2,8,2 |
| (m) Aluminium, Al | (n) Silicon, Si | (o) Phosphorus, P | (p) Sulfur, S | (q) Chlorine, Cl | (r) Argon, Ar |
| 2,8,3 | 2,8,4 | 2,8,5 | 2,8,6 | 2,8,7 | 2,8,8 |
| (s) Potassium, K | (t) Calcium, Ca | | | | |
| 2,8,8,1 | 2,8,8,2 | | | | |

4. (a) (i) 3
       (ii) 8
   (b) (i)  (ii)
   (c) (i) Lithium atom loses outer electron to become a singly positively charged lithium ion Li$^+$
       (ii) Oxygen atom gains 2 electrons to become a doubly negatively charged oxide ion O$^{2-}$
   (d)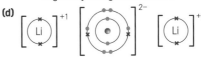
   (e) The lithium atom transfers one electron to the chlorine atom to form one Li$^+$ ion and one Cl$^-$ ion.
5. A bond formed between two atoms; in which a pair of electrons is shared.
6. (a) (i) Electrons    (ii) Electrons
   (b) The forces between the hydrogen chloride molecules are weak.
7. (a)  (b)
   (c) A covalent bond
8. (a) Covalent
   (b)

| Substance | Structural formula | | |
|---|---|---|---|
| | (i) | (ii) | (iii) |
| Nitrogen | N≡N | N ⦂ N | .x<br>N.xN<br>.x |
| Ammonia | H–N–H<br>\|<br>H | H N H<br>H | H.xN.xH<br>.x<br>H |
| Water | O<br>H   H | H O H | H.xO.xH |
| Bromine | Br–Br | Br Br | Br.xBr |
| Methane | H<br>\|<br>H–C–H<br>\|<br>H | H<br>H C H<br>H | H<br>.x<br>H.xC.xH<br>.x<br>H |
| Chlorine | Cl–Cl | Cl Cl | Cl.xCl |

9. (a) (i) Diamond
   (ii) Graphite
   (iii) Buckminster fullerene
   (b) Each carbon atom forms four covalent bonds in a very rigid giant structure.
   (c) Each carbon atom forms three covalent bonds in layers with free electrons able to move between the layers.
   (d) It has a layered structure in which the layers can pass over one another.
10. (a) Each silicon atom forms four covalent bonds to oxygen atoms, which in turn form two covalent bonds to silicon atoms in a very rigid giant structure.
    (b) Covalent bonding between oxygen and silicon atoms.
11. (a) 1 000 000
    (b) Nanoparticles have a huge surface area and can be attached to carbon nanotubes. The catalyst would then have an increased surface area.
    (c) In a scanning electron microscope, the electrons interact with the atoms that make up the sample surface, allowing an image of the atoms at the surface to be produced; The probe tip is extremely sharp – just one or two atoms at its point. There is a small electric voltage on the probe tip that can be used to move individual atoms.
    (d) Increased reactivity; Larger surface area.
12. (a) Nanocomposite polymers can have carbon nanotubes in that make them very strong; so have different applications to ordinary plastics, such as reinforcing tennis rackets, as well as making stronger and lighter building materials.
    (b) To carry drug molecules; To trap dangerous substances in the body and remove them; Catalysts because of huge surface area; Lubricants.
13. (a) Heat-proofing; electrical insulator
    (b) Plastic bags; clothing; toys; ropes
    (c) Increase conductivity of a solution; as a solvent or lysis agent; buffer solutions
    (d) To provide inert atmospheres; can be used to make electrical insulating materials
    (e) Lubricants; drill bit coatings; tools
    (f) Microchips; drug delivery catalysts

## Atomic Structure, Analysis and Quantitative Chemistry (pp 42–46)

1. (a) 4 = mass number; He = chemical symbol; Helium = element name; 2 = atomic number.
   (b) 2
   (c) 4
   (d) 2
   (e) 2
   (f) (i) Magnesium
       (ii) Oxygen
       (iii) Chlorine
       (iv) Titanium
2. Co: 27, 32, 27, Cobalt
   F: 9, 10, 9, Fluorine
   Mg: 12, 12, 12, Magnesium
   Fe: 26, 30, 26, Iron
   O: 8, 8, 8, Oxygen
   P: 15, 16, 15, Phosphorus
   Ar: 18, 22, 18, Argon
3. Atom of the same element with the same number of protons but different numbers of neutrons.
4. (a) Same atomic number and different mass numbers.
   (b) $^{12}_{6}C$: 6; 6; 6 (1 mark)
       $^{14}_{6}C$: 6; 8; 6 (1 mark)
5. (a) 23
   (b) 40
   (c) 63.5
   (d) 16
   (e) 1
   (f) 27
   (g) 48

(h) 80
(i) 14
6. (a) 18
   (b) 100
   (c) 160
   (d) 44
   (e) 74
   (f) 132
7. (a) The atom economy of a process tells you the proportion of atoms in the reactants; that become part of a useful product.
   (b) Atom economy = $100 \times \dfrac{\text{mass of atoms in desired product}}{\text{mass of atoms in reactants}}$
8. **Any three from:** Loss of products in: Weighing (inaccurately); Filtration (small amounts stay on filter paper); Loss in evaporation (some chemicals evaporate into the room); Loss in transferring liquids (small amounts stick to the side of the beaker); Loss during heating (some chemicals may evaporate).
9. (a) The reaction is reversible.
   (b) (i) From air
       (ii) **Any one from:** Cracking oil fractions or natural gas; Electrolysis of water.
   (c) Rate increases but yield decreases as the forward reaction is endothermic.
10. Percentage yield = $100 \times \dfrac{\text{Actual yield}}{\text{Predicted yield}}$
11. 100%; More efficient/More product
12. (a) Spitting from evaporating basin; Transferring solution from beaker.
    (b) Yield would be reduced.
    (c) 75%
    (d) (i) 80%
        (ii) 87.5%
        (iii) 95%
        (iv) 135g
        (v) 200kg

## Rates of Reaction (pp 47–51)

1. (a) Anita
   (b) It is measuring small changes in mass.
   (c) (i)–(iii)

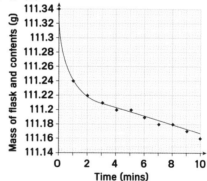

   (d) 111.23g (1 mark for correct number, 1 for correct unit)
   (e) Carbon dioxide is a product of the reaction; It is a gas and is lost to the atmosphere; The rate of a reaction can be determined by the rate of formation of a product; The faster carbon dioxide is produced, the greater the rate of reaction.
   (f) The rate will decrease over time; As the hydrochloric acid is used up, its concentration decreases.
   (g) When the surface is powdered, more surface and more particles are exposed to the acid; increasing the number of fruitful collisions.
   (h) The rate would increase; The speed of the particles increases/they collide more often/higher energy/increases the number of fruitful collisions.
   (i) The same method as for the marble chips, but use the same volume; of at least 3; different concentrations of acid; All other variables to remain the same.
   (j) Increase

**(k)** Increasing the concentration of reactants in a solution increases the number of reactant particles available; This increases the frequency of fruitful collisions.

**2. (a)** increases; rate; reducing; minimum; specific; small
*(All correct = 4 marks; 4–5 correct = 3 marks; 2–3 correct = 2 marks; 1 correct = 1 mark)*

**(b)** B

**(c) (i)** Oxygen ($O_2$); Gas syringe.

**(ii)** The amount of product depends on the amount of reactants. The same amount of product is formed from the same amount of reactants irrespective of rate; If the amount of reactants remains the same then so will the product; The catalyst lowers the amount of energy needed for successful collisions, but once all the reactants are used up the reaction will stop.

**(d)** Weigh the Manganese (IV) oxide before the reaction; Carry out the reaction; Dry the Manganese (IV) oxide; Reweigh the Manganese (IV) oxide after the reaction is completed. It should be the same.

**(e)** Manufacture of nitric acid – Platinum; Hydrogen peroxide ⟶ water + oxygen – Manganese (IV) oxide; Manufacture of ammonia – Iron; Catalytic converters for car exhausts – Platinum; Oxidation of ammonia – Platinum.

**(f)** To reduce costs.

**(g)** High pressure could cause the reaction vessel to split/explode, which could be dangerous; Expensive to build tanks/pipes to withstand the high pressure.

## Exothermic and Endothermic Reactions (pp 52–55)

**1. (a) (i)** C–H, O=O

**(ii)** C=O, O–H

**(b) (i)** Exothermic

**(ii)** Endothermic

**(c) (i–iii): Any three from:** Combustion reactions of fuels; Most polymerisation reactions; The setting of cement and concrete; Adding water to anhydrous copper (II) sulfate; Neutralization reactions such as direct reaction of acid and base; Adding concentrated acid to water; Burning of a substance; The thermite reaction; Reactions taking place in a self-heating can based on lime and aluminium; Many corrosion reactions such as oxidation of metals; The Haber-Bosch process of ammonia production.

**(d) (i)** Endothermic

**(ii)** The energy content of the reactants is less than that of the products; As the reaction proceeds, the overall energy increases.

**2. (a) Endothermic** – Potassium chloride and water; Sodium carbonate and ethanoic acid; Photosynthesis; Heating calcium carbonate; Electrolysis; Ammonium nitrate and barium hydroxide.
**Exothermic** – Magnesium and sulfuric acid; Copper (II) sulfate and magnesium; Calcium oxide and water; Thermite.
*(All correct = 5 marks; 8–9 correct = 4 marks; 6–7 correct = 3 marks; 2–5 correct = 2 marks; 1 correct = 1 mark)*

**(b)** The environment/surroundings

**(c)** Exothermic – Metals with acids; Neutralisation. Endothermic – Electrolysis; Photosynthesis.

**(d)** A drop in the temperature.

**(e)** A chemical reaction; that gives out energy.

**3. (a) (i)** $NH_4NO_3(s)$; Endothermic reaction/cools on dissolving in water.

**(ii)** $CaCl_2(s)$; Exothermic reaction heats/warms on dissolving in water.

**(b) (i) Any one from:** Produces a gas – could split the pack; Produces excess water – could split the pack.

**(ii)** Cools too much – the temperature drops to below freezing point of water (may drop to −30°C).

**4. (a) (i)** hydrated copper sulfate ⟶ anhydrous copper sulfate + water

**(ii)** anhydrous copper sulfate + water ⟶ hydrated copper sulfate

**(iii)** Yes. The forward reaction has to be heated. It takes in energy, so is endothermic; The reverse reaction is exothermic and gives out heat; If a reaction is exothermic in one direction, then it will be endothermic in the opposite direction. The same amount of energy is transferred in each case.

**(b)** $CuSO_4 \cdot 5H_2O(s) \rightleftharpoons CuSO_4(s) + 5H_2O(g)$
*(1 mark for correct formulae, 1 for balancing)*

**(c)** Measure the temperature using the thermometer; Temperature increases – exothermic reaction. Temperature decreases – endothermic reaction.

**(d)** Replace the polystyrene cup with a glass/metal container, e.g. boiling tube; Fill with water and heat from below.

**(e) Any two from:** More frequent readings; Can record over a long period for slow reactions; Less errors due to human error in readings; Greater resolution than thermometer; Can be in a sealed reaction.

## Acids, Bases and Salts (pp 56–58)

**1. (a)** acidic; alkali; greater; oxide; hydroxide

**(b)** A base is the oxide or hydroxide of a metal. It reacts with an acid to form a salt and water. An alkali is a base that is soluble in water.

**(c)** acid + base ⟶ salt + water

**(d)** Water

**(e)** Neutralisation

**(f)** hydrogen/$H^+(aq)$/$H_3O^+(aq)$

**(g)** $OH^-(aq)$

**(h)** $H^+(aq) + OH^-(aq) \longrightarrow H_2O(l)$ / $H_3O^+(aq) + OH^-(aq) \longrightarrow 2H_2O(l)$
*(1 mark for correct ions, 1 mark for balancing)*

**2. (a)** Sulfuric acid

**(b)** Copper carbonate in excess; Final solution not acidic after evaporation.

**(c)** Filtration

**(d) (i)** The copper sulfate contains water of crystallisation; Evaporation to dryness would produce some anhydrous copper sulfate.

**(ii)** Copper metal not reactive enough.

**(e) Any one from:** magnesium; aluminium; zinc; iron

**3. (a) Any soluble lead salt, e.g.:** lead nitrate.
**Any soluble iodide, e.g.:** potassium iodide.

**(b) (i)** A and B named salts from a); C = lead iodide; D = salt from anion and cation mentioned in a).

**(ii)** Mix the two solutions (better to have soluble iodide in excess); Filter the solution; Wash the precipitate of lead salt in the filter paper; Allow it to dry.

**(iii)** Lead salts are toxic.

## Electrolysis (pp 59–63)

**1.** ions; electric current; electrolysis; gain / lose; electrodes; neutral; Positively; negatively
*(All correct = 5 marks; 6–7 correct = 4 marks; 4–5 correct = 3 marks; 2–3 correct = 2 marks; 1 correct = 1 mark)*

**2. (a) (i)** X = Chlorine

**(ii)** Y = Hydrogen

**(b)** ions; reduction; atoms; molecules; oxidation; molecules
*(All 6 correct = 4 marks; 4–5 correct = 3 marks; 2–3 correct = 2 marks; 1 correct = 1 mark)*

**3. (a)** A – Carbon lining as cathode; B – Solution of aluminium oxide in molten cryolite; C – Steel tank; D – Molten aluminium

**(b)** To lower the melting point.

**(c)** React with oxygen; to produce carbon dioxide.

**(d) This is a model answer that would score full marks.**
Aluminium oxide is dissolved in molten cryolite, or aluminium oxide is melted. Aluminium ions are attracted to the negative electrode (cathode). At the negative electrode, aluminium ions gain electrons, or aluminium is formed. Oxide ions are attracted to the positive electrode (anode). Oxide ions lose electrons or oxygen is formed. Oxygen reacts with the carbon (electrode) to form carbon dioxide. Carbon dioxide is formed at the positive electrode (anode).

**(e)** negative; (reduction); negatively; (oxidation); ions; reactivity
(*All 6 correct = 3 marks; 3–5 correct = 2 marks; 1–2 correct = 1 mark*)

**(f)** Copper plating; Silver plating.
(*Both correct = 1 mark*)

**4. (a) (i)** It only allows the sodium ions through it.
**(ii)** NaOH (Sodium hydroxide)
**(b)** The chlorine produced is corrosive.
**(c)** There isn't any chlorine; at the cathode.

**5.** Cathode: $Al^{3+} + 3e^- \longrightarrow Al$ *(2 marks)*
Anode: $2O^{2-} \longrightarrow O_2(g) + 4e^-$ *(2 marks)*

**6.** $2Cl^- \longrightarrow Cl_2 + 2e^-$
(*1 for correct formula, and 1 for balancing*)

## Forces and their Effects (pp 64–72)

**1. (a)** 34 000 000N
**(b)** When two objects interact they exert an equal and opposite force on each other.
**(c)** $W = m \times g$
$W = 3\,000\,000 \times 10$;
$W = 30\,000\,000$N
**(d)** Resultant force = 34 000 000 − 30 000 000;
= 4 000 000N;
$F = m \times a$;
$a = \dfrac{4\,000\,000}{3\,000\,000}$; = 1.33m/s²
**(e)** It would travel in a straight line; at constant speed (constant velocity).

**2. (a)** 1000 − 800 − 100 − 100;
= 0 Newtons
**(b)** Travelling at a constant speed
**(c)** The car will slow down; because of friction/air resistance.
**(d)** The force from the engine is balanced; by friction/air resistance.
**(e) Any two from:** Lighter/lower mass; More streamlined/aerodynamic; More powerful engine

**3.** A – Stopped; B – Low constant speed; C – Higher constant speed.

**4. This is a model answer that would score full marks.** A bullet fired from a gun leaves at high velocity. This is shown by a steep line on a distance-time graph. When the bullet hits a solid wall, it decelerates quickly and comes to a stop. This is shown on the graph by a horizontal line.

**5. (a)** A – Constant speed; B – Speeding up;
C – Slowing down.
**(b)** velocity

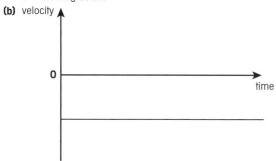

(*1 mark for horizontal line; 1 mark for negative velocity*)

**6. (a)** It is the distance a vehicle travels before the brakes are applied.
**(b)** The age of the driver; The speed of the car; If the driver had been drinking alcohol.
**(c)** It is the distance a vehicle travels after the brakes are applied.
**(d)** The speed of the car; The mass of the car; If the brakes are worn.
**(e)** The greater the speed; the greater the force needed.

**7. (a)** bigger; accelerates; balanced; terminal; smaller; decelerates.
**(b)** Force R is caused by drag/air resistance; Force W is caused by the effect of gravity on the mass/force (W is the weight).
**(c)** Falling in a dive position; Increasing mass; Jumping from high altitude where the air is thinner. (*Only accept 3 ticked boxes.*)
**(d)** A dive position is more streamlined so reduces drag; Increasing the mass increases the force of gravity/weight; Thinner air produces less drag.

**8. (a)**

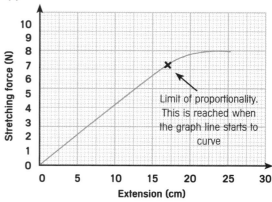

Limit of proportionality. This is reached when the graph line starts to curve

**(b) Any two from:** Can check for reproducibility; It allows anomalies to be detected and removed from the results; Improves results.
**(c)** The extension of the spring.
**(d)** Continuous
**(e)** Elastic potential energy/strain
**(f)** $k = \dfrac{F}{e}$; $= \dfrac{7.5}{0.25}$; = 30N/m

**9. (a)** Stopped
**(b)** $\dfrac{40}{80}$ = 0.5 m/s (*1 mark for calculation, 1 for correct answer*)
**(c)** Section D−E
**(d)** The shopper is moving in the opposite direction to that which they were walking in earlier.

**10. (a)** 25m/s
**(b)** $\dfrac{20}{60}$ = 0.33 m/s² (*1 mark for calculation, 1 for correct answer*)
**(c)** Distance = area under the graph; $= 25 \times \dfrac{240}{2}$;
= 3000m
**(d)** Distance = area under the graph; $= 25 \times 120$;
= 3000m

## The Kinetic Energy of Objects (pp 73–78)

**1. (a)** $W = m \times g = 1000 \times 10$; = 10 000N
**(b)** $W = F \times d$; = 10 000 × 1.5; = 15 000J
(*1 mark for correct answer, 1 mark for correct units*)
**(c)** $P = \dfrac{E}{t}$; $= \dfrac{15000}{3}$; = 5000W (5kW)
(*1 mark for correct answer, 1 mark for correct units*)
**(d)** 15 000J

**2. (a)** The lorry
**(b)** It has a greater mass.

**3. (a)** $E_k = \dfrac{1}{2} mv^2$; $= \dfrac{1}{2} \times 1500 \times 20^2$; = 750 × 400;
= 300 000J
**(b)** $W = F \times d$; 300 000 = 10 000 × distance;
distance $= \dfrac{300\,000}{10\,000}$; = 30m
**(c)** It has been converted into heat energy; by friction in the brakes.

**4. (a) (i)** $E_p = m \times g \times h$; = 100 × 10 × 2; = 2000J
**(ii)** $P = \dfrac{E}{t} = 2000J \dfrac{2}{s} = 1000W$
**(b)** 2000J
**(c)** $E_k = \dfrac{1}{2} mv^2$; 2000 = $\dfrac{1}{2} \times 100 \times v^2$;
$v^2 = \dfrac{4000}{100}$; v = 6.32 m/s

**5. (a)** The lorry
**(b)** 1200 × 10; = 12 000 kg m/s
**(c)** $\dfrac{12000}{300}$; = 40 m/s (90 mph)

**6.** $E_k = \dfrac{1}{2}mv^2 = \dfrac{1}{2} \times 1000 \times (20)^2 = 200\,000J$

**7.** $E_k = \dfrac{1}{2}mv^2 = \dfrac{1}{2} \times 3200 \times (10)^2 = 1\,600\,000J$

8. **(a)** Yes

   **(b) Any three from:** The satellite is changing direction, so its velocity is changing; Momentum = mass × velocity; On one side of the Earth, it is travelling with a positive momentum; On the other side it is going in the opposite direction so its momentum is negative.

9. During a collision, momentum is conserved; Total momentum before must be the same as afterwards; The balls have the same mass, so when one loses all its momentum by stopping, the other one must gain the same momentum; and therefore the same speed.

10. On impact, some of the kinetic energy of the car is used to deform the crumple zone; The crumple zone increases the time in which the change of momentum takes place; This reduces the forces on the occupants of the car.

11. Momentum before gun is fired = momentum after gun is fired $(1000 × 12) + (1200 × 10)$; = $2200 × v$; $12\,000 +$

    $12\,000$; = $2200 × v$; $\dfrac{24\,000}{2200} = v$; $v = 10.9\text{m/s}$

12. **(a)** Every force has an equal and opposite reaction; Momentum is conserved.

    **(b)** Momentum before gun is fired = momentum after; Momentum of bullet = $350 × 0.01$; = $3.5\text{kgm/s}$ Momentum of gun = $-3.5\text{kgm/s}$; $-3.5 = 1 × v$; $v = -3.5\text{m/s}$; The gun moves backwards at $3.5\text{m/s}$.

## Currents in Electrical Circuits (pp 79–82)

1. **(a)** Some of the outer electrons in the jumper are transferred onto the balloon. Therefore the balloon is charged.

   **(b)** The balloon gains negative charge and repels electrons away from the wall; This leaves the wall positively charged and so the balloon remains attracted to the wall.

2. Like; repel; unlike; attract (*1 mark for getting like-repel combination and 1 mark for the unlike-attract combination*)

3. Air I; Rubber I; Water C; Metals C; Plastic I; Skin C. (*3 marks for all correct, 2 marks for 4–5 correct, 1 mark for 2–3 correct*).

4. **(a)** It controls the current through the device.

   **(b)** In series

5. A diode – 3; A resistor at constant temperature – 1; A filament lamp – 2 (*2 marks for all three correct, 1 mark for 1–2 correct*)

6. **(a)** $I = \dfrac{V}{R} = \dfrac{4}{2} = 2\Omega$ or $I = \dfrac{V}{R} = \dfrac{2}{1} = 2\Omega$

   (*1 mark for the calculation involving $\dfrac{4}{2}$ and / or $\dfrac{2}{1}$, 1 mark for stating the units*)

   **(b)** A resistor at constant temperature

   **(c)** A 2; B 4; C 1; D 3.

7. **(a)**

   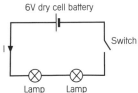

   6V dry cell battery

   Switch

   I

   Lamp    Lamp

   (*1 mark for showing correct symbols for battery, lamp and switch, 1 mark for showing lamps in series, 1 mark for showing current direction, 1 mark for showing a completed circuit (no gaps)*).

   **(b)**

   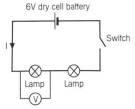

   6V dry cell battery

   Switch

   I

   Lamp    Lamp

   V

   **(c)** 3 volts

   **(d)** Total resistance = $10\Omega + 10\Omega = 20\Omega$ for resistances in series; V = IR gives: $I = \dfrac{V}{R}$; $= \dfrac{6}{20} =$ 0.3A (*1 mark for calculating the total resistance of $20\Omega$, 1 mark for re-arranging V = IR to give*

$I = \dfrac{V}{R}$, *1 mark for calculating the numerical value of the current and giving its units in amps*)

   **(e)** $I = \dfrac{Q}{t}$ so that Q = I × t; = $0.3\text{A} × (2 × 60) = 36\text{C}$

   (*1 mark for using the correct equation $I = \dfrac{Q}{t}$ and re-arranging it to give Q = It, 1 mark for the correct calculation, 1 mark for stating the correct units as Coulombs*)

## Mains Electricity (pp 83–85)

1. **(a)** Direct current; 1.5 volts

   **(b)** Alternating current; accept between 230 and 240 volts

   **(c)** (*3 marks if all seven correct, −1 for each incorrect*)

   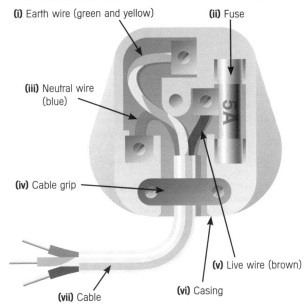

   **(i)** Earth wire (green and yellow)        **(ii)** Fuse

   **(iii)** Neutral wire (blue)

   **(iv)** Cable grip

   **(v)** Live wire (brown)

   **(vii)** Cable        **(vi)** Casing

   **(d)** Melts if too high a current occurs.

   **(e)** $I = \dfrac{P}{V} = \dfrac{1150}{230} = 5.0\text{A}$; so 5A fuse needed

   (*1 mark for using the correct version of the equation, 1 mark for the correct calculation and units*)

2. **(a)** $P = \dfrac{E}{t}$

   $E = P × t$

   $E = 60\text{W} × (2 × 3600)\text{s}$

   $= 432\,000\text{J}$ (*1 mark for using the correct equation after re-arranging, 1 mark for correct calculation and units*)

   **(b)** The remaining energy is used to heat the filament; The light bulb gets hot, this is wasted energy; Fluorescent lights use less energy and are more efficient.

   **(c)**

   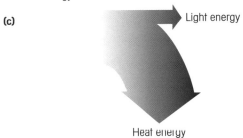

   Light energy

   Heat energy

   **(d)** $P = I × V$

   $I = \dfrac{P}{V}$

   $I = \dfrac{60\text{W}}{230\text{V}} = 0.26\text{A}$; so 3A fuse needed

   (*1 mark for using the correct equation after re-arranging, 1 mark for correct calculation and units*)

**(e)** $E = V \times Q$

$Q = \dfrac{E}{V} = \dfrac{432\ 000\text{J}}{230\text{V}} = 1878.3\ Coulombs$

= 1880 C (*1 mark for using the correct equation after re-arranging, 1 mark for calculating the energy required, 1 mark for giving correct units and 1 mark for giving answer to 3 s.f.*)

## The Decay of Radioactive Substances (pp 86–88)

1. **(a)**

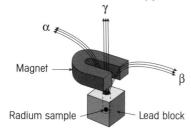

**(b) (i)** Positive charge of +2
   **(ii)** Negative charge of −1
   **(iii)** No charge
**(c)** All three types of radiation are stopped by lead; Alpha radiation is stopped by a few sheets of paper; Beta radiation is stopped by a sheet of aluminium (or equivalent); Gamma radiation is stopped effectively by several centimetres of lead.
2. **(a)** Two minutes (time taken to fall to half its value)
   **(b)** Reached background radiation levels.
3. **(a) Any suitable answer**, **e.g.:** Gamma-rays for killing cancer cells; Radiotherapy treatment.
   **(b) Any suitable answer**, **e.g.:** Gamma-rays for examining materials; Airport security.
4. **(a)** Beta radiation
   **(b)** Low penetrating power, causes damage to the skin and other living tissue.
5. **Any four from:** Radon gas; From food; Medical; Cosmic rays; From rocks; Nuclear industry
6. Because it occurs in very small doses.
7. **(a)** Number of protons is called the atomic number; Number of protons and neutrons is called the mass number (or atomic mass).
   **(b)** The emission of an electron from inside the nucleus.

**(c)** The time taken for half of the active nuclei to decay or radiation emitted to reach half original level.
**(d)** $a = 92$, $b = 234$, $c = 4$ and $d = 2$
**(e)** $e = 234$, $f = 234$, $g = 0$, $h = -1$

## Nuclear Fission and Nuclear Fusion (pp 89–92)

1. **(a)** Isotopes (of hydrogen)
   **(b)** 2 (contains 2 protons); 4 (2 neutrons and 2 protons)
2. They all contain 1 negative particle; Called the electron.
3. 1 (the number of protons)
4. Uranium; Plutonium
5. **(a)** A neutron
   **(b)** The fissionable material becomes unstable and splits into two smaller nuclei; A huge amount of energy is released; 2 or 3 further neutrons are also released.
   **(c)** A chain reaction
6.

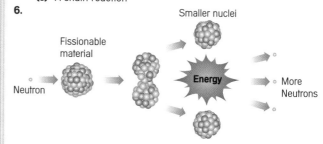

(*1 mark for showing neutron collision with nucleus, 1 mark for showing nucleus splitting, 1 mark for showing energy release or more neutrons*)
7. **(a)** The joining together of two small nuclei to form a larger nucleus; The release of a large amount of energy.
   **(b)** Hydrogen; Helium
   **(c)** Iron
8. main sequence; red giant; white dwarf; black dwarf
9. **(a)** Supernova
   **(b)** Neutron star and black hole
10. Energy is released in the form of heat; Each reaction releases energy.
11. **(a)** Nuclear fission
    **(b)** Nuclear fusion powers the Sun.
    **(c)** Waste products may be radioactive with long half-lives.

**(g)** The three students repeated the experiment, but they used powdered marble instead of marble chips. The rate of reaction between the calcium carbonate and the hydrochloric acid was much faster with the powder. Explain why increasing the surface area of pieces of a solid also increases the rate of reaction. **(2 marks)**

**(h)** The students decided to investigate the effect of temperature on the rate of reaction. Predict what effect temperature would have on the rate of reaction. Explain why. **(2 marks)**

**(i)** To complete their work, the students investigated the effect of the concentration of the acid. Describe how they could do this. **(4 marks)**

**(j)** If they increased the concentration of the acid, what would happen to the rate of reaction? Tick the correct answer. **(1 mark)**

Stay the same ◯

Decrease ◯

Increase ◯

**(k)** Explain why. **(2 marks)**

**2.** **(a)** Fill in the missing words to complete the following sentences. (4 marks)

A catalyst is a substance that ............................... the ............................... of a

chemical reaction, without being used up in the process. Catalysts work by ...............................

the activation energy, the ............................... energy needed for the reaction to happen.

Catalysts are ............................... . Different reactions need different catalysts. Because a

catalyst is not used up in a reaction, only very ............................... amounts are needed.

**(b)**

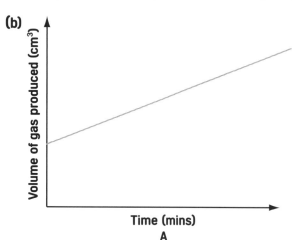

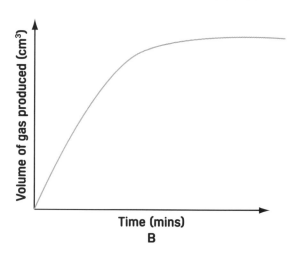

Which of the two graphs shows the addition of a catalyst? (1 mark)

.......................................................................................................................................

**(c)** Use the equation below to answer the questions.

hydrogen peroxide ⟶ water + oxygen

$2H_2O_2(aq)$ ⟶ $2H_2O(l)$ + $O_2(g)$

The rate of this reaction can be measured by collecting one of the products.

**(i)** Which product would you collect and how would you collect it? (2 marks)

.......................................................................................................................................

**(ii)** If a catalyst is added to the reaction, the same volume of oxygen is produced in total, but the
reaction happens a lot faster. Explain why. (3 marks)

.......................................................................................................................................

.......................................................................................................................................

.......................................................................................................................................

.......................................................................................................................................

**(d)** Describe how you could show that the catalyst Manganese (IV) oxide was chemically unchanged by the reaction? **(4 marks)**

........................................................................................................................................................................

........................................................................................................................................................................

........................................................................................................................................................................

........................................................................................................................................................................

**(e)** Draw straight lines to match the reactions in list A to the catalysts in list B. **(4 marks)**

**List A**                                                        **List B**

| Manufacture of nitric acid |

| Hydrogen peroxide ⟶ water + oxygen |

| Manufacture of ammonia |

| Catalytic converters for car exhausts |

| Oxidation of ammonia |

| Catalase |

| Iron |

| Manganese (IV) oxide |

| Platinum |

**(f)** Why are catalysts used in industrial processes? Tick the correct answer. **(1 mark)**

To reduce the amount of reactants needed.  ◯

To reduce the amount of products produced.  ◯

To reduce costs.  ◯

To employ chemists.  ◯

**(g)** Increasing the pressure of reacting gases increases the frequency of collisions and so increases the rate of reaction.

In the Haber process a pressure of 200 atmospheres is used. Why isn't a higher pressure used, even though it would produce a fast reaction rate? **(2 marks)**

........................................................................................................................................................................

........................................................................................................................................................................

**(Total: ............ / 45 marks)**

**1.** **(a)** The equation below shows the reaction of methane burning in oxygen.

$$CH_4 + 2O_2 \longrightarrow CO_2 + 2H_2O$$

   **(i)** Which chemical bonds are broken? (1 mark)

   _____

   **(ii)** Which chemical bonds are made? (1 mark)

   _____

**(b)** What is the name given to a chemical reaction that:

   **(i)** gives out heat? (1 mark)

   _____

   **(ii)** takes in heat? (1 mark)

   _____

**(c)** Give **three** examples of exothermic reactions. (3 marks)

   **(i)** _____

   **(ii)** _____

   **(iii)** _____

**(d)** The energy diagram below shows the energy change in a chemical reaction.

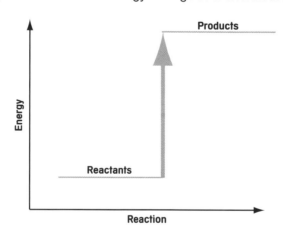

   **(i)** Is the reaction endothermic or exothermic? (1 mark)

   _____

   **(ii)** How do you know? (2 marks)

   _____

   _____

**2.** **(a)** Which of the following reactions are exothermic and which are endothermic? Put ticks in the correct columns (Endothermic or Exothermic). (5 marks)

| Reaction | Endothermic | Exothermic |
|---|---|---|
| Magnesium and sulfuric acid | | |
| Potassium chloride and water | | |
| Sodium carbonate and ethanoic acid | | |
| Photosynthesis | | |
| Copper(II) sulfate and magnesium | | |
| Calcium oxide and water | | |
| Heating calcium carbonate | | |
| Thermite | | |
| Electrolysis | | |
| Ammonium nitrate and barium hydroxide | | |

**(b)** In an endothermic change, the products have more energy than the reactants. Where does the energy come from? (1 mark)

**(c)** Draw straight lines to link the energy changes in list A to their corresponding examples in list B. (4 marks)

**List A**

Exothermic

Endothermic

**List B**

Metals with acids

Electrolysis

Neutralisation

Photosynthesis

**(d)** You can tell if a reaction is exothermic or endothermic by taking the temperature of the reaction. How would you know if the reaction was endothermic? (1 mark)

**(e)** Write a definition of 'exothermic'. (2 marks)

**3.** **(a)** Some sports injury packs are based upon endothermic reactions. A reactant is wrapped in a plastic tube. When the pack is hit against the body, the tube breaks and water mixes with the reactant. Hand warmer packs are similar but use a reaction that is exothermic.

The energy diagrams below show the energy change in two chemical reactions.

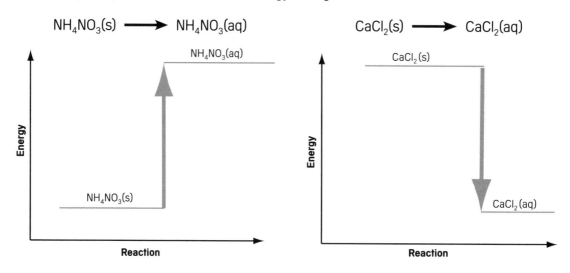

$$NH_4NO_3(s) \longrightarrow NH_4NO_3(aq)$$

$$CaCl_2(s) \longrightarrow CaCl_2(aq)$$

**(i)** Which reactant would you use for the sports injury cooling pack? Give a reason for your choice. (2 marks)

_____

_____

**(ii)** Which reactant would you use for the hand warmer pack? Give a reason for your choice. (2 marks)

_____

_____

**(b)** The following reactions are endothermic. Give a reason why they are not used in sports injury packs.

**(i)** $Na_2CO_3(s) + 2CH_3COOH(aq) \longrightarrow 2CH_3COONa(aq) + CO_2 + H_2O$ (1 mark)

_____

_____

**(ii)** $Ba(OH)_2.8H_2O(s) + 2NH_4NO_3(s) \longrightarrow Ba(NO_3)_2(s) + 2NH_3(aq) + 10H_2O(l)$ (1 mark)

_____

_____

**4.** **(a)** The equation below shows a reversible reaction.

hydrated copper sulfate ⇌ anhydrous copper sulfate + water

(blue) (white)

**(i)** Which reaction is endothermic? (1 mark)

_____

**(ii)** Which reaction is exothermic? (1 mark)

_____

**(iii)** Is the same amount of energy transferred in each case? Explain your answer. (3 marks)

_____

_____

_____

**(b)** Write a balanced symbol equation for the reaction. (2 marks)

_____

**(c)** How could you use the apparatus below to determine if a reaction was endothermic or exothermic? (2 marks)

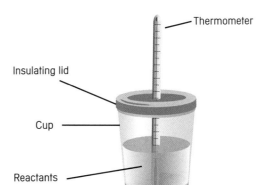

Thermometer

Insulating lid

Cup

Reactants

_____

_____

_____

_____

**(d)** How could you change the apparatus so that you could determine the energy released by burning a fuel? (2 marks)

_____

_____

**(e)** Describe the advantages of using sensors and a data logger to take readings of the temperature changes in a chemical reaction. (2 marks)

_____

_____

**(Total: _____ / 42 marks)**

**1.** Adam the gardener has been growing potatoes in his garden.

The potatoes like to grow in a sour soil with a low pH, usually about 5.5. He has had a good crop of potatoes and now he wants to grow some cabbages. The cabbages like a sweet soil with a pH of about 7.5.

He can change the pH of his soil by adding lime.

**(a)** Complete the following sentences.                                        (5 marks)

Adam's soil has a pH of 5.5 so it is described chemically as ............................ . Lime is an

example of an ............................ . It has a pH ............................ than 7.

These compounds are usually the ............................ or ............................ of metals.

**(b)** Explain the difference between an alkali and a base.                      (1 mark)

.................................................................................................................................

.................................................................................................................................

**(c)** Write a general word equation for the reaction of an acid with a base.   (1 mark)

.................................................................................................................................

**(d)** What is the name of the molecule that is always formed in this reaction? (1 mark)

.................................................................................................................................

**(e)** What name is given to these reactions when acids and bases react with each other?  (1 mark)

.................................................................................................................................

**(f)** Which ion do **all** acids contain?                                       (1 mark)

.................................................................................................................................

**(g)** Which ion is found in **all** alkalis?                                    (1 mark)

.................................................................................................................................

**(h)** Write an ionic equation (with states) for these two ions reacting.       (2 marks)

.................................................................................................................................

.................................................................................................................................

**2.** Amanda and Jay are preparing copper sulfate crystals in their school laboratory.

I think copper carbonate would be better in excess

I think it would be better to have the acid in excess

**(a)** Name the acid they would use to prepare copper sulfate from copper carbonate. (1 mark)

.........................................................................................................................................

**(b)** Explain which of the two reactants you think it would be better to have in excess. (2 marks)

.........................................................................................................................................

.........................................................................................................................................

**(c)** State the method for removing the excess component. (1 mark)

.........................................................................................................................................

**(d)** Amanda and Jay heated the copper sulfate solution to evaporate off **most** of the water, but then they stopped the heating.

    **(i)** Explain why they did **not** evaporate the solution to dryness. (2 marks)

.........................................................................................................................................

.........................................................................................................................................

    **(ii)** Why could they not make copper sulfate from copper metal and dilute acid? (1 mark)

.........................................................................................................................................

**(e)** Some of the class were making a salt using metal and acid. Name a metal that would be suitable for reacting with dilute acid. (1 mark)

.........................................................................................................................................

**3.** Lead iodide $PbI_2$(s) is insoluble in cold water and can be made by mixing two soluble salts.

**(a)** Name a soluble lead salt and a soluble iodide salt. (2 marks)

.................................................................................................................................

.................................................................................................................................

**(b)** The diagram shows the steps involved in preparing lead iodide.

**(i)** Name the substances **A**, **B**, **C** and **D**. (4 marks)

**A:** .........................................................................................................................

**B:** .........................................................................................................................

**C:** .........................................................................................................................

**D:** .........................................................................................................................

**(ii)** Describe how to carry out this preparation. (4 marks)

.................................................................................................................................

.................................................................................................................................

.................................................................................................................................

.................................................................................................................................

**(iii)** **C** can be washed to remove lead ions from solution. Why would you want to remove lead ions? (1 mark)

.................................................................................................................................

**(Total:** ............ **/ 32 marks)**

1. Fill in the missing words to complete the following sentences. (5 marks)

   When an ionic substance is melted or dissolved in water, the _____ are free to move about in the liquid or solution. Passing an _____ through ionic substances that are molten, for example lead bromide, or in solution, breaks them down into elements. This process is called _____. During electrolysis, ions _____ electrons at the _____, forming electrically _____ atoms or molecules, which are then released. _____ charged ions move to the negative electrode and _____ charged ions move to the positive electrode.

2. (a) The diagram below shows the electrolysis of sodium chloride solution.

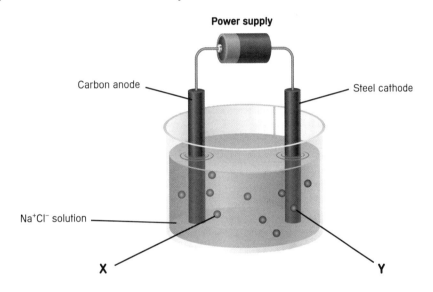

**Power supply**

Carbon anode

Steel cathode

Na⁺Cl⁻ solution

X

Y

   Identify the two gases: (2 marks)

   (i) X: _____

   (ii) Y: _____

   (b) Complete the sentences by filling in the missing words: (4 marks)

   Hydrogen _____ gain electrons in a process called _____ to form hydrogen _____. The hydrogen atoms combine to form _____ of hydrogen gas.

   Chloride ions lose electrons in a process called _____ to form chlorine atoms. The chlorine atoms combine to form _____ of chlorine gas.

   The overall reaction is: $2NaCl_{(aq)} + 2H_2O_{(l)} \longrightarrow 2Na^+_{(aq)} + 2OH^-_{(aq)} + Cl_{2(g)} + H_{2(g)}$

**3.** Read the following information and then answer the questions.

---

Aluminium must be obtained from its ore by electrolysis because it is too reactive to be extracted by heating with carbon. The steps in the process are:

**1.** Aluminium ore (bauxite) is purified to leave aluminium oxide.

**2.** Aluminium oxide is mixed with cryolite.

**3.** The aluminium oxide and cryolite mixture is melted.

**4.** A current is passed through the molten mixture.

The equation for the electrolysis of aluminium oxide is:

aluminium oxide $\longrightarrow$ aluminium $+$ oxygen

$2Al_2O_3(l)$ $\quad\quad\quad 4Al(l)$ $+$ $3O_2(g)$

The diagram shows the apparatus used to electrolyse aluminium oxide.

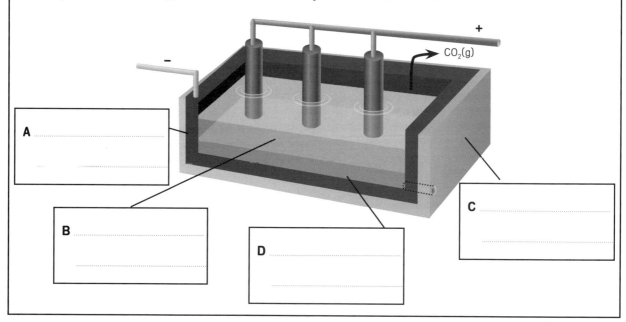

**A** .............

**B** .............

**D** .............

**C** .............

---

**(a)** Fill in boxes **A–D** on the diagram. (4 marks)

**(b)** Why is cryolite added to the bauxite? (1 mark)

.....................................................................................................................................

**(c)** Why do the positive electrodes have to be frequently replaced? (2 marks)

.....................................................................................................................................

**(d)** *In this question you will be assessed on using good English, organising information clearly and using scientific terms where appropriate.*

Explain how aluminium and carbon dioxide are formed in the process. Refer to the diagram and the equation. (6 marks)

**(e)** Complete the sentences using the words provided. (3 marks)

| ions | reactivity | (oxidation) | negatively | (reduction) | negative |
|------|-----------|-------------|------------|-------------|----------|

At the ........................ electrode, positively charged ions gain electrons

........................ and at the positive electrode, ........................ charged ions lose

electrons ........................ . If there is a mixture of ........................ , then the

products formed depend on the ........................ of the elements involved.

**(f)** Tick all of the applications of electroplating that are accurate. (1 mark)

Copper plating ◯

Silver plating ◯

Plastic plating ◯

**4.** **(a)** In industry, a more complicated electrolysis cell is used.

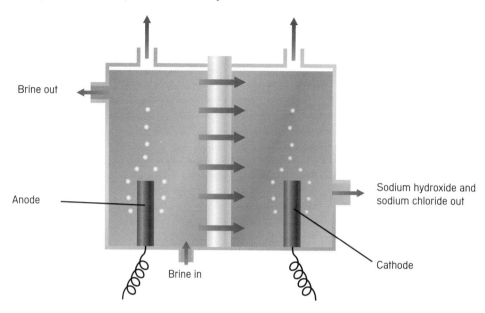

At the cathode, hydrogen in the water is reduced to hydrogen gas, releasing hydroxide ions into the solution: $2H_2O + 2e^- \longrightarrow H_2 + 2OH^-$

The non-permeable ion exchange membrane at the centre of the cell allows the sodium ions ($Na^+$) to pass to the second chamber, where they react with the hydroxide ions to produce sodium hydroxide (NaOH).

The overall reaction for the electrolysis of brine is: $2NaCl + 2H_2O \longrightarrow Cl_2 + H_2 + 2NaOH$

**(i)** Why is the membrane needed? (1 mark)

........................................................................................................................

**(ii)** Which product is used to make soap? (1 mark)

........................................................................................................................

**(b)** The anode has to be made from a non-reactive metal such as titanium. Why is this? Tick the box next to the correct answer.

The hydrogen produced is flammable. ◯

The sodium hydroxide is highly toxic. ◯

The chlorine produced is corrosive. ◯

Carbon anodes are too expensive. ◯

**(c)** Complete the following sentence: (2 marks)

The cathode can be made from nickel because ..................................................................

........................................................................................................................

**(Total:** .......... **/ 32 marks)**

**5.** Aluminium is the most abundant metallic element in the Earth's crust. It is never found in free, metallic form, and it was once considered a precious metal more valuable than gold.

In the industrial electrolysis of molten aluminium, aluminium metal and oxygen gas are produced. Write half equations for what happens at each electrode. (4 marks)

**Cathode:** .......................................................................................................

**Anode:** .......................................................................................................

**6.** Use the equation below to write the half equation for the reaction occurring at the anode. (2 marks)

$$2NaCl_{(aq)} + 2H_2O_{(l)} \longrightarrow 2Na^+_{(aq)} + 2OH^-_{(aq)} + Cl_{2(g)} + H_{2(g)}$$

**(Total:** ............ **/ 6 marks)**

1.   In 1969, the Apollo 11 mission was launched. The Saturn V rocket that powered the Apollo mission had a mass of 3 000 000kg and exerted a downwards force on the air behind it of 34 000 000N.

(a) How big is the upwards force of the air on the rocket?                                    (1 mark)

(b) Explain how you worked out your answer to part (a).                                     (1 mark)

(c) Calculate the weight of the rocket (g = 10N/kg). Select the correct formula from the
     equation sheet.                                                                                         (2 marks)

(d) By using the equation sheet and your answers to parts (a) and (c), find the resultant force on the
     rocket and hence its acceleration at launch.                                                    (5 marks)

(e) Once the Apollo mission spacecraft had escaped the Earth's gravity, the engines shut off and there
     was no resultant force on it. Describe the spacecraft's motion at this point.            (2 marks)

2. The diagram shows the forces acting on a car driving along a road.

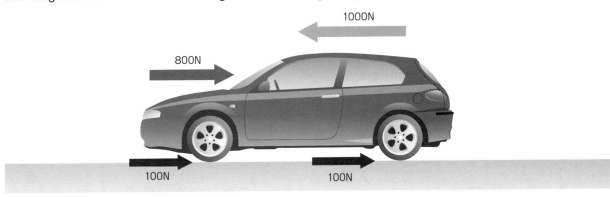

1000N

800N

100N          100N

**(a)** Calculate the resultant force on the car. Show clearly how you work out your answer. (2 marks)

........................................................................................................................

........................................................................................................................

**(b)** Which statement best describes the car's motion? Tick the box next to the correct answer.

(1 mark)

| | |
|---|---|
| Travelling at a constant speed | |
| Stopped | |
| Accelerating | |
| Decelerating | |

**(c)** The driver takes his foot off the accelerator, so the engine is no longer providing a force. How will this affect the motion of the car? (2 marks)

........................................................................................................................

........................................................................................................................

**(d)** The driver accelerates until the car reaches its maximum speed. Describe the forces once the car is at its top speed. (2 marks)

........................................................................................................................

........................................................................................................................

**(e)** A second car has a higher top speed. Suggest **two** things that may be different about the second car. (2 marks)

........................................................................................................................

........................................................................................................................

3.  Distance–time graphs can be used to represent the motion of an object.

    Match the graphs to the correct descriptions of motion. Draw a line from each graph to its corresponding motion. (3 marks)

**Distance–time graph**          **Description of motion**

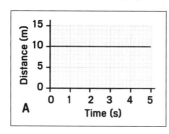

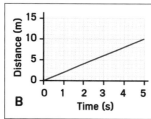

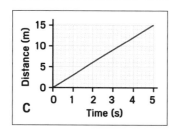

Low constant speed

Higher constant speed

Speeding up

Stopped

4.  *In this question you will be assessed on using good English, organising information clearly and using scientific terms where appropriate.*

    Describe the motion and shape of a distance–time graph that would be produced by a bullet fired from a gun into a solid wall, from the time it leaves the gun to the point when it stops in the wall. (6 marks)

**5.** **(a)** Velocity–time graphs can be used to represent the motion of an object.

Match the graphs to the correct descriptions of motion.

Draw a line from each graph to its corresponding motion. (3 marks)

**Velocity–time graph**        **Description of motion**

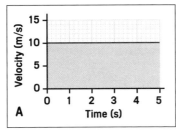

A

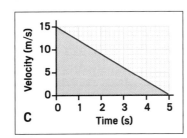

B

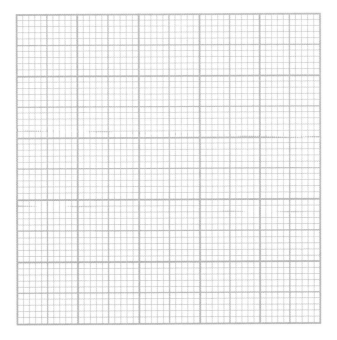

C

Slowing down

Constant speed

Speeding up

Stopped

**(b)** How would an object travelling backwards at a constant speed be shown on a velocity–time graph? Draw a graph to show this. (2 marks)

**6.** The diagram below shows the thinking and braking distance of a car.

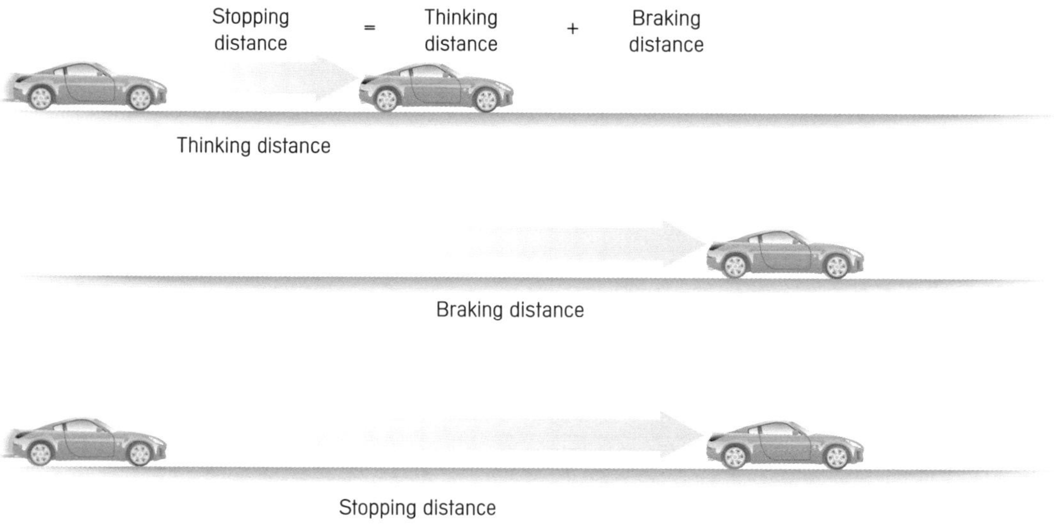

| Stopping distance | = | Thinking distance | + | Braking distance |

Thinking distance

Braking distance

Stopping distance

**(a)** What is meant by the thinking distance? (1 mark)

**(b)** Tick the boxes next to the options below that would affect the thinking distance. (3 marks)

| | |
|---|---|
| The age of the driver | |
| The speed of the car | |
| If the driver had been drinking alcohol | |
| The mass of the car | |
| If the brakes are worn | |

**(c)** What is meant by the braking distance? (1 mark)

**(d)** Tick the boxes next to the options below that would affect the braking distance. (3 marks)

| | |
|---|---|
| The age of the driver | |
| The speed of the car | |
| If the driver had been drinking alcohol | |
| The mass of the car | |
| If the brakes are worn | |

**(e)** What is the connection between the speed of the vehicle and the size of the force needed to stop it in a certain distance? (2 marks)

......................................................................................................................

......................................................................................................................

**7.** The diagram shows the forces acting on a skydiver.

**(a)** Use the words in the table below to fill in the spaces in the following sentences.

| bigger | smaller | terminal |
|--------|---------|----------|
| accelerates | decelerates | balanced |

When the skydiver first jumps out of the plane, force W is ............................... than force

R and the skydiver ............................... . (1 mark)

The forces on the skydiver in the diagram are ..............................., which means that he is at his

............................... velocity. (1 mark)

When the parachute is opened, force W is ............................... than force R and the

skydiver ............................... . (1 mark)

**(b)** State what causes forces R and W. (2 marks)

......................................................................................................................

......................................................................................................................

**(c)** A skydiver is attempting to break the freefall speed record. Which of the following would help to increase his terminal velocity? Tick the boxes next to the correct options. (3 marks)

| | |
|---|---|
| Falling in a dive position | |
| Jumping from a faster airplane | |
| Increasing mass | |
| Jumping from high altitude where the air is thinner | |

**(d)** Explain your answer to **(c)**. (3 marks)

........................................................................................................

........................................................................................................

........................................................................................................

**8.** An experiment was carried out to investigate the force needed to stretch a spring.

Weights were gradually added to the spring and the extension of the spring was measured.
The experiment was carried out three times and the average results plotted on the graph below.

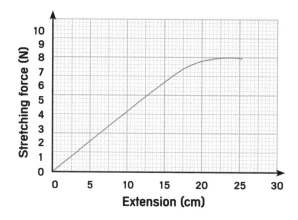

**(a)** On the graph, mark the limit of proportionality with a cross. (1 mark)

**(b)** What is the benefit of repeating the experiment three times? (2 marks)

........................................................................................................

........................................................................................................

**(c)** In the experiment, what was the dependent variable? (1 mark)

........................................................................................................

**(d)** Is this variable continuous, categoric or ordered? (1 mark)

........................................................................................................

**(e)** When the force is applied to the spring, what type of energy is stored in the spring? (1 mark)

........................................................................................................

**(f)** Use the graph and the equation sheet to calculate the spring constant. Give the unit. (3 marks)

........................................................................................................

........................................................................................................

........................................................................................................

**(Total: .............. / 64 marks)**

9. The graph below is a distance–time graph for a person doing their shopping.

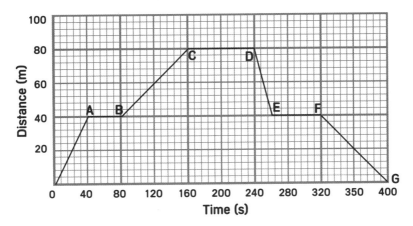

**(a)** Describe the motion in the region C–D. (1 mark)

...................................................................................................................................................

**(b)** Calculate the speed in section B–C. (2 marks)

...................................................................................................................................................

...................................................................................................................................................

**(c)** During what section of the journey is the person travelling at the fastest speed? (1 mark)

...................................................................................................................................................

**(d)** In which direction are they travelling at this point? (1 mark)

...................................................................................................................................................

**10.** The graph below is a velocity–time graph for a train.

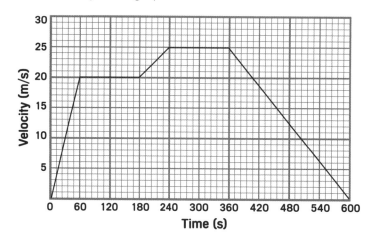

**(a)** What is the maximum velocity reached by the train? (1 mark)

..................................................................................................................................................

**(b)** Calculate the maximum acceleration of the train. (2 marks)

..................................................................................................................................................

..................................................................................................................................................

**(c)** Calculate the distance travelled by the train in the last four minutes of its journey. (3 marks)

..................................................................................................................................................

..................................................................................................................................................

..................................................................................................................................................

**(d)** Calculate the distance travelled by the train while it is travelling at its fastest speed. (3 marks)

..................................................................................................................................................

..................................................................................................................................................

..................................................................................................................................................

**(Total:** .............. **/ 14 marks)**

1. A forklift truck at a warehouse is used to lift pallets of bricks with a total mass of 1000kg.

**(a)** Calculate the weight of each pallet of bricks. (Take g = 10N/kg). (2 marks)

........................................................................................................................

........................................................................................................................

**(b)** When lifting the pallets onto a high shelf, the forklift truck raises the pallets through a height of 1.5m. Calculate the work done on the pallets by the forklift truck. Give the unit. (4 marks)

........................................................................................................................

........................................................................................................................

........................................................................................................................

**(c)** If it takes three seconds to lift the pallet, what is the power being delivered by the motor? Give the unit. (4 marks)

........................................................................................................................

........................................................................................................................

........................................................................................................................

**(d)** By how much does lifting the pallets increase their gravitational potential energy? (1 mark)

........................................................................................................................

........................................................................................................................

**2.** A car and a lorry are both travelling at the same speed.

**(a)** Which vehicle has the greatest kinetic energy? (1 mark)

**(b)** Explain your answer to **(a)**. (1 mark)

**3.** A car travels along a road at a constant speed of 20m/s.

**(a)** If the car has a mass of 1500kg, what is the kinetic energy of the car? (4 marks)

**(b)** To stop the car, the brakes must do work on the car. The driver applies the brakes, which provide a constant braking force of 10kN. How far will the car travel before it stops? (4 marks)

**(c)** Once the car has come to a halt, what has happened to its kinetic energy? (2 marks)

4.  When weight lifting, chemical energy in the muscles is converted to gravitational potential energy in the weights.

(a) The weightlifter shown above lifts a 100kg mass to a height of 2 metres.

(i) How much gravitational potential energy is gained by the weights? (g = 10N/kg)          (3 marks)

(ii) If the lift takes two seconds, what power is delivered by the weightlifter?          (2 marks)

(b) On completion of the lift, the weights are dropped. How much kinetic energy do they have just before they hit the floor?          (1 mark)

(c) Calculate the speed at which the weights hit the floor.          (4 marks)

**5.** The diagram shows a number of different vehicles all travelling at the same speed.

**(a)** Which of the vehicles will have the greatest momentum? (1 mark)

**(b)** The car in the diagram has a mass of 1200kg and is travelling at a speed of 10m/s.
Calculate the momentum of the car. (2 marks)

**(c)** The motor cycle has a mass of 300kg. If the motor cycle now increases its velocity so that it has the same momentum as the car, how fast must it be going? (2 marks)

**6.** A car of mass 1000kg moves along a road at a constant speed of 20m/s.
Calculate its kinetic energy. (2 marks)

**7.** A truck of mass 32 000kg moves along a road with a speed of 10m/s.
Calculate its kinetic energy. (2 marks)

**8.** A satellite in orbit around the Earth travels at a constant speed.

**(a)** Is its momentum changing? (1 mark)

..............................................................................................................................................................

**(b)** Explain your answer to part **(a)**. You may wish to use a diagram. (3 marks)

..............................................................................................................................................................

..............................................................................................................................................................

..............................................................................................................................................................

..............................................................................................................................................................

**9.** During a game of snooker, when one ball hits another, if one ball stops the other continues at the same speed as the first ball. Explain why this happens. (4 marks)

..............................................................................................................................................................

..............................................................................................................................................................

..............................................................................................................................................................

..............................................................................................................................................................

**10.** One of the key safety features of any car is the crumple zone. By referring to energy and momentum, explain how a crumple zone helps to protect the occupants of the car from injury. (3 marks)

..............................................................................................................................................................

..............................................................................................................................................................

..............................................................................................................................................................

..............................................................................................................................................................

..............................................................................................................................................................

..............................................................................................................................................................

**11.** Two cars are travelling in the same direction along a road. Car A collides with car B and they lock together. Calculate their velocity after the collision. (6 marks)

BEFORE:
A
12m/s
1000kg

B
10m/s
1200kg

AFTER:
A    B
→ v

**12.** The diagram shows a bullet being fired from a gun.

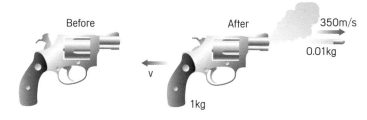

Before

After    350m/s
0.01kg

v

1kg

**(a)** In the 'After' diagram, the gun is seen to be moving backwards. Why does this happen? (2 marks)

**(b)** Calculate the recoil velocity of the gun. (6 marks)

**(Total: ........ / 67 marks)**

1.  When an inflated balloon is rubbed against a woolly jumper and placed against a vertical wall, it remains fixed to the wall.

   **(a)** Explain what happens to the balloon when it is rubbed by the jumper.                    (1 mark)

   ........................................................................................................................................................

   **(b)** Explain why the balloon sticks to the wall.                    (2 marks)

   ........................................................................................................................................................

   ........................................................................................................................................................

   ........................................................................................................................................................

2.  Use the words in the box below to complete the following sentences.                    (2 marks)

   | unlike | repel | attract | like |
   |---|---|---|---|

   When two electrically charged objects are brought together they exert a force on each other.

   ........................................... charges ........................................... and ...........................................

   charges therefore ...........................................

3.  Below is a list of six materials. Three are good conductors of electricity and three are poor conductors of electricity, called insulators. In the boxes provided, indicate whether each material is a conductor (C) or an insulator (I).                    (3 marks)

   Air ◯

   Rubber ◯

   Water ◯

   Metals ◯

   Plastic ◯

   Skin ◯

**4.** The following circuit is used to investigate the current-potential difference characteristics of various electronic components.

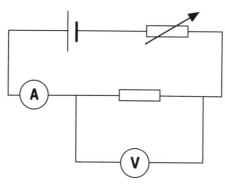

**(a)** What is the purpose of the variable resistor (known as a rheostat) in the circuit? (1 mark)

.................................................................................................................................................

**(b)** Is the ammeter shown in the circuit connected in parallel or connected in series with the unknown resistor? (1 mark)

.................................................................................................................................................

**5.** The current–potential difference results for three electrical devices are shown in the graphs below. Which graph corresponds to each of the components listed below? Enter the appropriate graph numbers in the boxes provided. (2 marks)

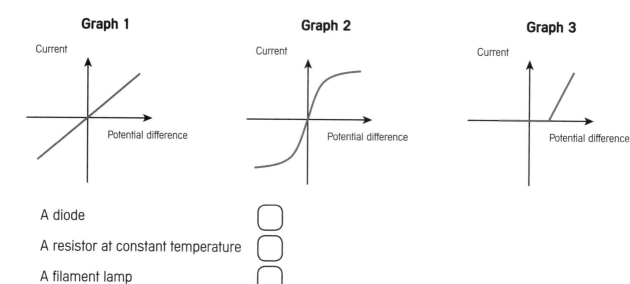

A diode ☐

A resistor at constant temperature ☐

A filament lamp ☐

**6.** In a set of measurements, a potential difference of 4 volts was recorded for a current of 2 amps, and 2 volts for a current of 1 amp.

**(a)** Calculate the value of the resistance of the device. Give the units of resistance.　　　(2 marks)

........................................................................................................................

........................................................................................................................

**(b)** Which device or devices show a constant resistance? Circle the correct answer.　　　(1 mark)

A diode

A resistor at constant temperature

A filament lamp

**(c)** Match the components numbered **1–4** with statements **A**, **B**, **C** and **D** below. Write the number of the component next to the appropriate statement.　　　(4 marks)

**1** Light dependent resistor (LDR)

**2** Thermistor

**3** Diode

**4** Filament lamp

**A** Resistance decreases as the temperature of the component increases. ☐

**B** Resistance increases as the temperature of the component increases. ☐

**C** Resistance decreases as light intensity increases. ☐

**D** The component has a very high resistance in one direction. ☐

**7.** A simple circuit is being constructed using a 6 volt dry-cell battery, two small lamps and a switch. The two lamps are connected in series.

**(a)** Draw a circuit diagram in the box below to show this particular arrangement. Indicate the direction of the current. Label your diagram clearly. (4 marks)

**(b)** The potential difference across the first lamp is to be measured. Indicate on your circuit diagram the position and connections required for the voltmeter. (1 mark)

**(c)** If both lamps are identical, what is the value of the potential difference across the first lamp? (1 mark)

**(d)** The resistance of each lamp is 10Ω. Calculate the current flowing in the circuit. (3 marks)

**(e)** When the switch is closed, the lamps remain 'on' for two minutes. Calculate the amount of electric charge that flows through the circuit in this time. State the units. (3 marks)

**(Total:** ............ **/ 31 marks)**

**1.** A dry-cell battery is connected to an oscilloscope and the following trace is observed. Each square on the diagram represents 1cm x 1cm.

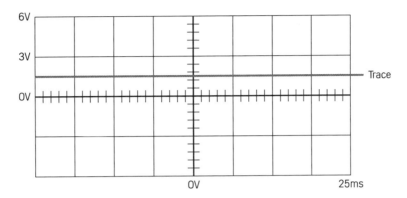

The x sensitivity is 6.25ms/cm and the y sensitivity is 3V/cm

**(a)** Determine from the trace the value of the potential difference of the dry-cell battery and the type of current generated. **(1 mark)**

.......................................................................................................................................................................

**(b)** The dry-cell battery is replaced by the mains voltage and the trace recorded on the oscilloscope as shown.

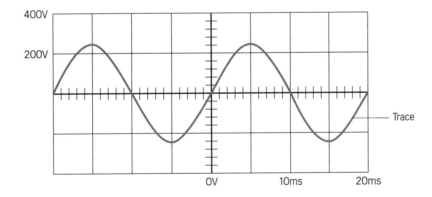

The x sensitivity is 5ms/cm (5 × 10⁻³s/cm) and the y sensitivity is 200V/cm

Determine the value of the potential difference in this case (from the amplitude of the wave) and the type of current generated. **(2 marks)**

.......................................................................................................................................................................

.......................................................................................................................................................................

**(c)** The alternating current is used to provide power to a vacuum cleaner via a three-pin plug. On the following diagram, label the key components of the three-pin plug using the boxes provided. (3 marks)

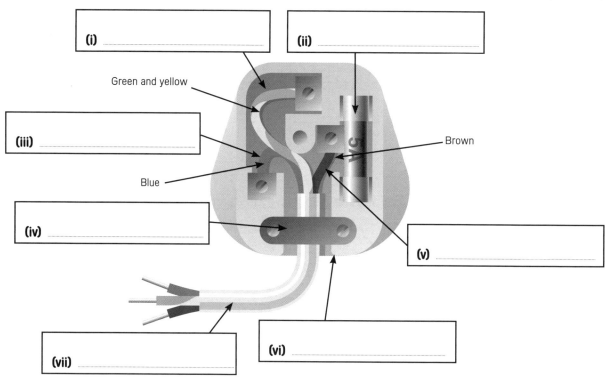

(i) ........................................

(ii) ........................................

Green and yellow

(iii) ........................................

Brown

Blue

(iv) ........................................

(v) ........................................

(vi) ........................................

(vii) ........................................

**(d)** What is the purpose of the fuse? (1 mark)

........................................................................................................................

**(e)** If the power of the vacuum cleaner is 1000W and the mains is 230 volts, calculate the rating of the fuse that should be used in the three-pin plug. Fuse ratings available are 3A, 5A and 15A. (2 marks)

........................................................................................................................

**2.** An ordinary 60W light bulb is used to light a small area of a room and is switched on for two hours.

**(a)** Calculate the energy transferred in this time. (2 marks)

........................................................................................................................

........................................................................................................................

**(b)** Filament light bulbs, like the one mentioned above, are not very efficient. In fact less than 10% of the electrical energy is converted into light energy. Explain what happens to the rest of the energy. Suggest a possible replacement lighting device. (3 marks)

........................................................................................................................

........................................................................................................................

........................................................................................................................

**(c)** Draw a Sankey diagram for the 60W light bulb. (2 marks)

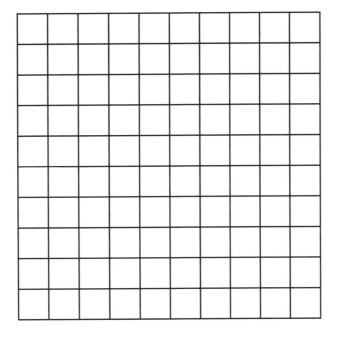

**(d)** The light bulb uses the mains supply of 230 volts. Calculate the size of the fuse that should be used in the three-pin plug. Fuse ratings available are 3A, 5A and 15A. (2 marks)

........................................................................................................................

........................................................................................................................

........................................................................................................................

**(Total: ............. / 18 marks)**

### Higher Tier

**(e)** When the light is switched on for two hours, calculate the amount of charge that flows through the bulb.

Give your answer to **three** significant figures. Remember to give the units. (4 marks)

........................................................................................................................

........................................................................................................................

........................................................................................................................

........................................................................................................................

**(Total: ............. / 4 marks)**

1. A small sample of radioactive radium is placed in the centre of a lead container. A tiny hole allows the radiation to be emitted vertically. Above the hole a small magnet is positioned as shown in the diagram.

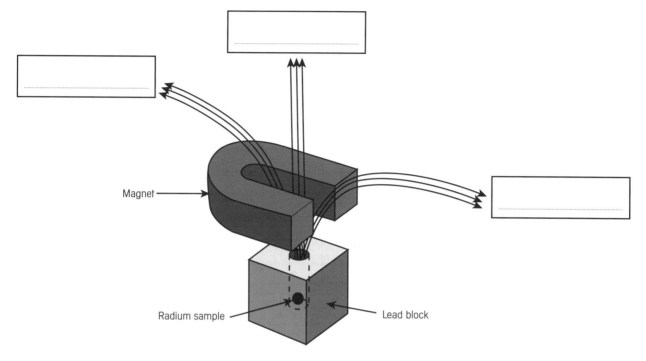

Magnet

Radium sample          Lead block

**(a)** The diagram shows the emission of alpha, beta and gamma radiation. Label the diagram to indicate the type of radiation emitted in the boxes provided.                                      (3 marks)

**(b)** What are the charges on each of these emissions?                                      (3 marks)

**(i)** Alpha radiation: ..................................................................................................................

**(ii)** Beta radiation: ..................................................................................................................

**(iii)** Gamma radiation: ..................................................................................................................

**(c)** Why is very little radiation emitted to the side or below the container? Comment on the penetrating power of each type of radiation in your answer.                                      (4 marks)

..................................................................................................................................................

..................................................................................................................................................

..................................................................................................................................................

..................................................................................................................................................

..................................................................................................................................................

**2.** A small sample of radioactive material was collected and tested in a laboratory. When first tested, the count rate from the sample was 1000 counts per second and it fell to 250 counts per second after four minutes.

**(a)** What is the half-life of the material? (1 mark)

.................................................................................................................................................

**(b)** After a few hours the count rate was eight counts per minute and remained constant. What caused the count rate to become constant? (1 mark)

.................................................................................................................................................

**3.** There are a number of uses for radioactive materials.

**(a)** Name or briefly describe **one** medical use of a radioactive material. (1 mark)

.................................................................................................................................................

**(b)** Name or briefly describe **one** industrial use of a radioactive material. (1 mark)

.................................................................................................................................................

**4.** The damage caused by radiation to a human body depends on a number of factors, such as the type of radiation a person is exposed to and where the source of radiation is located in relation to the body.

**(a)** Which type(s) of radiation are most dangerous outside the body? (1 mark)

.................................................................................................................................................

**(b)** Why is this? (1 mark)

.................................................................................................................................................

**5.** Name **four** sources that contribute to background radiation. (3 marks)

.................................................................................................................................................

.................................................................................................................................................

**6.** Explain why background radiation poses a very low risk to our health. (1 mark)

.................................................................................................................................................

**7.** The graph shows part of the decay of uranium (U) into thorium (Th). The long arrows pointing to the left show alpha decays and the short arrows pointing to the right show beta decays. The element Pa is palladium.

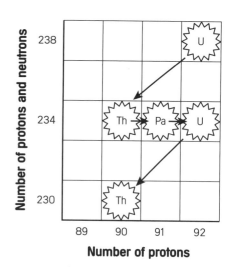

**(a)** With reference to the graph, what are the names usually given to the 'number of protons' and the 'number of protons plus the number of neutrons' in the above diagram? (2 marks)

........................................................................................................................................................................

........................................................................................................................................................................

**(b)** Thorium itself decays by beta emission. What is beta decay? (1 mark)

........................................................................................................................................................................

**(c)** Both of the decay processes, alpha decay and beta decay, involve nuclei with a different half-life. What is meant by the term 'half-life'? (1 mark)

........................................................................................................................................................................

**(Total: ............. / 24 marks)**

---

**Higher Tier**

**(d)** Complete the nuclear equation for the decay of uranium-238 into thorium-234 by alpha decay, by stating the values of *a, b, c* and *d*. $^{238}_{a}U \longrightarrow ^{b}_{90}Th + ^{c}_{d}He$ (2 marks)

........................................................................................................................................................................

........................................................................................................................................................................

**(e)** Complete the nuclear equation for the decay of thorium-234 by beta emission, indicating the values of *e, f, g* and *h*. $^{e}_{90}Th \longrightarrow ^{f}_{91}Pa + ^{g}_{h}e$ (2 marks)

........................................................................................................................................................................

........................................................................................................................................................................

**(Total: ............. / 4 marks)**

1. In a nuclear fusion reaction the elements tritium and deuterium are used.

   They are both derived from the simplest element, hydrogen, and have similar properties since they all contain one proton in the nucleus.

   **(a)** What is the name given to atoms like tritium and deuterium? (1 mark)

   ......................................................................................................................................

   **(b)** In the fusion reaction, the elements of deuterium and tritium combine to form a new element called helium, as well as releasing a neutron. The helium produced is also electrically neutral.

   What is the atomic number of helium and how many particles are contained in the nucleus? (2 marks)

   ......................................................................................................................................

   ......................................................................................................................................

2. Hydrogen, deuterium and tritium are all electrically neutral.

   How many negative particles do each of these elements have and what is the name given to this particle? (2 marks)

   ......................................................................................................................................

   ......................................................................................................................................

3. Hydrogen has no neutrons and one proton, deuterium has one neutron and one proton and tritium has two neutrons and one proton.

   What is the atomic number of deuterium? (1 mark)

   ......................................................................................................................................

4. In nuclear fission, there are two fissionable materials in common use in nuclear power stations.

   What are these **two** materials? (2 marks)

   ......................................................................................................................................

   ......................................................................................................................................

**5.** In order for nuclear fission to occur, the fissionable material must first absorb a particular type of particle.

    **(a)** What is the name given to this particle?     (1 mark)

    **(b)** When fission takes place, three further processes occur after the particle is absorbed. Describe these **three** processes.     (3 marks)

    **(c)** If further collisions occur, a particular type of process takes place. What is this process called?     (1 mark)

**6.** In the space below, draw a sketch of a nuclear fission process, labelling the main processes and particles involved, that leads to continual energy release.     (3 marks)

**7.** The picture shows an image of the Sun, which has a surface temperature of over 5800°C.
The process that keeps the Sun burning is known as nuclear fusion.

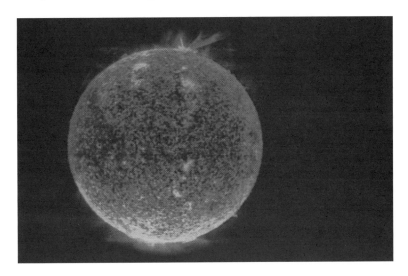

**(a)** What does nuclear fusion involve? (2 marks)

..........................................................................................................................................

..........................................................................................................................................

**(b)** In the fusion process within the Sun, what element is being fused and what element is being
formed? (2 marks)

..........................................................................................................................................

**(c)** During this stable phase of the Sun's life history, other elements are also being formed.
What is the final element that is made within a star's interior? (1 mark)

..........................................................................................................................................

**8.** Complete the following sentence about the life history of a star, like the Sun.

At the end of the stable period it leaves the ............................................................... to

become a ...................................................................., followed by a period when it becomes a

............................................ and finally a ................................

............................................. (4 marks)

**9.** For stars that are much larger than the Sun, their life history is very different.

**(a)** What is the name given to the huge explosion that follows the red supergiant phase? (1 mark)

..........................................................................................................................................

**(b)** Give the names of the objects that may be left after this explosion. (2 marks)

..........................................................................................................................................

# P2 Nuclear Fission and Nuclear Fusion

10. Which of the following statements about uranium fission are true?
    Tick the **two** correct options. (2 marks)

    Energy is released in the form of heat. ⬭

    Heat energy is taken in. ⬭

    Each reaction releases energy. ⬭

    Each reaction involves heavy nuclei. ⬭

    **(Total: _____ / 30 marks)**

## Higher Tier

11. The nuclear equation below shows a reaction that takes place in the core of a nuclear reactor.

$$^{235}_{92}U + {}^{1}_{0}n \longrightarrow {}^{95}_{39}Y + {}^{138}_{53}I + 3{}^{1}_{0}n$$

   **(a)** What is the name of the reaction that is taking place? (1 mark)

   _____

   **(b)** What is the difference between this type of reaction and the one that powers our own Sun? (1 mark)

   _____

   **(c)** What long-term problems may be caused by the waste products of this reaction? (1 mark)

   _____

   _____

   **(Total: _____ / 3 marks)**

# Notes

# Chemistry Data Sheet

1.  **Reactivity Series of Metals**

| | |
|---|---|
| Potassium | most reactive |
| Sodium | |
| Calcium | |
| Magnesium | |
| Aluminium | |
| *Carbon* | |
| Zinc | |
| Iron | |
| Tin | |
| Lead | |
| *Hydrogen* | |
| Copper | |
| Silver | |
| Gold | |
| Platinum | least reactive |

(elements in italics, though non-metals, have been included for comparison)

2.  **Formulae of Some Common Ions**

| Positive ions | | | Negative ions | |
|---|---|---|---|---|
| **Name** | **Formula** | | **Name** | **Formula** |
| Hydrogen | $H^+$ | | Chloride | $Cl^-$ |
| Sodium | $Na^+$ | | Bromide | $Br^-$ |
| Silver | $Ag^+$ | | Fluoride | $F^-$ |
| Potassium | $K^+$ | | Iodide | $I^-$ |
| Lithium | $Li^+$ | | Hydroxide | $OH^-$ |
| Ammonium | $NH_4^+$ | | Nitrate | $NO_3^-$ |
| Barium | $Ba^{2+}$ | | Oxide | $O^{2-}$ |
| Calcium | $Ca^{2+}$ | | Sulfide | $S^{2-}$ |
| Copper (II) | $Cu^{2+}$ | | Sulfate | $SO_4^{2-}$ |
| Magnesium | $Mg^{2+}$ | | Carbonate | $CO_3^{2-}$ |
| Zinc | $Zn^{2+}$ | | | |
| Lead | $Pb^{2+}$ | | | |
| Iron (II) | $Fe^{2+}$ | | | |
| Iron (III) | $Fe^{3+}$ | | | |
| Aluminium | $Al^{3+}$ | | | |

# Physics Equation Sheet

|  |  |
|---|---|
| $a = \dfrac{F}{m}$ or $F = m \times a$ | $F$ resultant force<br>$m$ mass<br>$a$ acceleration |
| $a = \dfrac{v - u}{t}$ | $a$ acceleration     $u$ initial velocity<br>$v$ final velocity     $t$ time taken |
| $W = m \times g$ | $W$ weight<br>$m$ mass<br>$g$ gravitational field strength |
| $F = k \times e$ | $F$ force<br>$k$ spring constant<br>$e$ extension |
| $W = F \times d$ | $W$ work done<br>$F$ force applied<br>$d$ distance moved in the direction of the force |
| $P = \dfrac{E}{t}$ | $P$ power<br>$E$ energy transferred<br>$t$ time taken |
| $E_p = m \times g \times h$ | $E_p$ change in gravitational potential energy<br>$m$ mass<br>$g$ gravitational field strength<br>$h$ change in height |
| $E_k = \dfrac{1}{2} \times m \times v^2$ | $E_k$ kinetic energy<br>$m$ mass<br>$v$ speed |
| $p = m \times v$ | $p$ momentum<br>$m$ mass<br>$v$ velocity |
| $I = \dfrac{Q}{t}$ | $I$ current<br>$Q$ charge<br>$t$ time |
| $V = \dfrac{W}{Q}$ | $V$ potential difference<br>$W$ work done<br>$Q$ charge |
| $V = I \times R$ | $V$ potential difference<br>$I$ current<br>$R$ resistance |
| $P = \dfrac{E}{t}$ | $P$ power<br>$E$ energy<br>$t$ time |
| $P = I \times V$ | $P$ power<br>$I$ current<br>$V$ potential difference |
| $E = V \times Q$ | $E$ energy<br>$V$ potential difference<br>$Q$ charge |
| $T = \dfrac{1}{f}$ | $T$ periodic time<br>$f$ frequency |

# Periodic Table

**Key**

| relative atomic mass |
| **atomic symbol** |
| name |
| atomic (proton) number |

| 1 | hydrogen | 1 |

| Group 1 | Group 2 | | | | | | | | | | | Group 3 | Group 4 | Group 5 | Group 6 | Group 7 | Group 0 |
|---|---|---|---|---|---|---|---|---|---|---|---|---|---|---|---|---|---|
| | | | | | | | | | | | | | | | | | 4 **He** helium 2 |
| 7 **Li** lithium 3 | 9 **Be** beryllium 4 | | | | | | | | | | | 11 **B** boron 5 | 12 **C** carbon 6 | 14 **N** nitrogen 7 | 16 **O** oxygen 8 | 19 **F** fluorine 9 | 20 **Ne** neon 10 |
| 23 **Na** sodium 11 | 24 **Mg** magnesium 12 | | | | | | | | | | | 27 **Al** aluminium 13 | 28 **Si** silicon 14 | 31 **P** phosphorus 15 | 32 **S** sulfur 16 | 35.5 **Cl** chlorine 17 | 40 **Ar** argon 18 |
| 39 **K** potassium 19 | 40 **Ca** calcium 20 | 45 **Sc** scandium 21 | 48 **Ti** titanium 22 | 51 **V** vanadium 23 | 52 **Cr** chromium 24 | 55 **Mn** manganese 25 | 56 **Fe** iron 26 | 59 **Co** cobalt 27 | 59 **Ni** nickel 28 | 63.5 **Cu** copper 29 | 65 **Zn** zinc 30 | 70 **Ga** gallium 31 | 73 **Ge** germanium 32 | 75 **As** arsenic 33 | 79 **Se** selenium 34 | 80 **Br** bromine 35 | 84 **Kr** krypton 36 |
| 85 **Rb** rubidium 37 | 88 **Sr** strontium 38 | 89 **Y** yttrium 39 | 91 **Zr** zirconium 40 | 93 **Nb** niobium 41 | 96 **Mo** molybdenum 42 | [98] **Tc** technetium 43 | 101 **Ru** ruthenium 44 | 103 **Rh** rhodium 45 | 106 **Pd** palladium 46 | 108 **Ag** silver 47 | 112 **Cd** cadmium 48 | 115 **In** indium 49 | 119 **Sn** tin 50 | 122 **Sb** antimony 51 | 128 **Te** tellurium 52 | 127 **I** iodine 53 | 131 **Xe** xenon 54 |
| 133 **Cs** caesium 55 | 137 **Ba** barium 56 | 139 **La*** lanthanum 57 | 178 **Hf** hafnium 72 | 181 **Ta** tantalum 73 | 184 **W** tungsten 74 | 186 **Re** rhenium 75 | 190 **Os** osmium 76 | 192 **Ir** iridium 77 | 195 **Pt** platinum 78 | 197 **Au** gold 79 | 201 **Hg** mercury 80 | 204 **Tl** thallium 81 | 207 **Pb** lead 82 | 209 **Bi** bismuth 83 | [209] **Po** polonium 84 | [210] **At** astatine 85 | [222] **Rn** radon 86 |
| [223] **Fr** francium 87 | [226] **Ra** radium 88 | [227] **Ac*** actinium 89 | [261] **Rf** rutherfordium 104 | [262] **Db** dubnium 105 | [266] **Sg** seaborgium 106 | [264] **Bh** bohrium 107 | [277] **Hs** hassium 108 | [268] **Mt** meitnerium 109 | [271] **Ds** darmstadtium 110 | [272] **Rg** roentgenium 111 | | | | | | | |

Elements with atomic numbers 112–116 have been reported but not fully authenticated

*The lanthanoids (atomic numbers 58–71) and the actinoids (atomic numbers 90–103) have been omitted.

The relative atomic masses of copper and chlorine have not been rounded to the nearest whole number.